PRACTICAL PARENTING™ TIPS

VICKI LANSKY

PRACTICAL PARENTING™ TIPS

Over 1,500 Helpful Hints for the First Five Years

Meadowbrook Press
Distributed by Simon & Schuster
New York

Special thanks go to Kathryn Ring, editor of *Practical Parenting* newsletter, for her help in editing the original version of this book.

Library of Congress Cataloging-in-Publication Data

Lansky, Vicki.
   [Practical parenting tips for the first five years]
   Vicki Lansky's practical parenting tips for the first five years
      p.   cm.
   ISBN 0-88166-192-9 (pbk.)
    1.   Child rearing—United States—Handbooks, manuals, etc.
  2.   Infants—Care—United States—Handbooks, manuals, etc.
  I.   Title.
   HQ769.L2454   1992
   649'.1–dc20   92-17149
                                              CIP

Simon & Schuster Ordering # 0-671-79205-9

Published by Meadowbrook Press, 18318 Minnetonka Boulevard, Deephaven, Minnesota 55391.

BOOK TRADE DISTRIBUTION by Simon & Schuster, a division of Simon and Schuster, Inc., 1230 Avenue of the Americas, New York, NY 10020.

Editors of the original edition: Kathryn Ring and Mary Holm
Editors of the 1992 edition: Kate Moore and Bonnie Gruen
Managing Editor: Kerstin Gorham
Editorial Director: Jay Johnson
Desktop Coordinator: Jon C. Wright
Art Director: Tabor Harlow
Production Coordinator: Matthew Thurber
Cover Design: MacLean and Tuminelly
Cover Art: Roberta Collier Morales

92 93 94 95 96 97   10 9 8 7 6 5 4 3 2 1

Printed in the United States of America

INTRODUCTION

My first child had the good grace to arrive at the end of May, so I was able to wheel him to the park almost daily. For him there was the fresh air and sunshine—for me there were the other new mothers on the park bench. It did not take me long to discover that their babies, too, revised their waking schedules nightly and were fussy in the evenings when adults longed for private time. To my relief, I found I didn't have the only child who hadn't read Dr. Spock!

Not only did I get support from these park bench mothers—I got a lot of ideas from them. These weren't the kind of ideas I read in baby care books or heard in the pediatrician's office. They were practical tips born of experience, so they seemed worth trying. Other mothers, I was finding, were a wonderful source of information.

Several years later I put together two cookbooks, *Feed Me! I'm Yours* and *The Taming of the C.A.N.D.Y. Monster*. Both were collections of recipes and feeding ideas that had worked for me and other parents. I am not a nutrition expert, but I do know what food is good for my kids and in what forms they will eat it. I simply shared what I felt were good ideas. The success of these two books continues to amaze me.

In 1979 I began publishing a newsletter called *Practical Parenting* because I still wanted to know more about what was working for other parents. Each issue of the newsletter includes a place for readers to answer questions posed by other parents. We asked parents to share their questions, recipes, tips, and experiences. So from the tips sent into the newsletter, from word of mouth from my experiences, from sources of all kinds, I have collected the best of child care tips that parents have shared for the first five years of living with children.

1992 Epilogue

The time has come once again to update and include the multitude of new parenting tips (actually over 400) shared with me by parents. Some are in response to my "HELP! Family Circle" column and my "Practical Parenting" column in the *Parents' Guide* that comes with *Sesame Street Magazine*, and others I've learned by reading about—and from listening to—parents. It was also necessary to eliminate information no longer relevant such as shag rug rakes; and add warnings about dangers such as babies getting trapped in the frames of waterbeds; and discuss helpful new products such as boxed drinks, diaper wraps, and room intercoms to monitor babies.

I still get excited when I learn a new tip that I wished I had known about before. I think there are many here that will make your life easier. While I hope you will find many you can use, do remember the most important tip of all:

WARNING!

This Book Can Be Hazardous to Your Mental Health If You Think You Must Try Every Idea Listed. Trying Them All May Lead to a Nervous Breakdown. Thinking You Should Is Guaranteed to Produce An Intense Case of Guilt.

Vicki Lansky

ACKNOWLEDGMENTS

My special thanks to the thousands of *Practical Parenting* newsletter subscribers who have taken the time to share tips, hints, and ideas that have worked for them and to contributors, too numerous to list here, who sent me tips after reading the first edition, plus those current contributors whose names have been added to our acknowledgments.

Nancy Addington
Vivian Adkins
L. Alexander
Sharon Amastae
Susan Anderson
Kenneth Andreas
Cathy Andrews
Carol Andruskiewicz
Marcia Ashodian
Beverly Audeh-Merrie
Gayle & Clifford Baker
Chester Ball, Jr.
Linda Ballirano
Francis Barker
Trudy Barr
Chris Baumgartner
Ina Belcher
Sarah Bell
Gail Berkove
Gloria Blaha
Jeanne Blasi
Carrie Bloedel
Barbara Bowen
Eric Bowman
Maureen Bozicevich
Barbara Brown
Julie Burrows
Cynthia Cade
Beadie Cambardella
Marjorie Cargill
Martha Carman
Eric Carroll
Nancy & Thomas
  Caswell
Marjorie Chamberlain
Lillian Cohen
Francie Conley
Marcia Conley
Mrs. M. Cooper
Madeleine Cotts
Donna & Dan
  Counselman
Gay Courter
Jeannine Daly
Jill & John DeGutis
Sandra Dewex
Bessie Dobbs
Gail Dodge
Beth Dooley
Gail Duke
Kay Dyer
Carol Eggers
Karen & Lawrence
  Evans
Abigail F. Farber, M.D.
Linda & Robert Fegan

Jerome Fishkin
Linda Fornelli
Debbie & Glenn
  Freeman
Shirley Gayer
Sandra Gingrich
Mrs. Ivan Grabhorn
Emily Grainger
Kathe Grooms
Marlene Gwiazdon
Jerry Hallfin
Mary Hallman
Mary Beth Hamann
Ann Handley
Lori & Steve Havran
Roberta Heeson
Fritz Heger
Eileen Helm
Gilda Henderson
Rhonda Hendrickson
Sharon Herpers
Diana Hestwood
Jeanne Hill
Jackie Hofhenke
Laurie Horstman
Kay Hunke
Karen Jenkins
Winnie Jones
Susan Jones
Vivian Jury
Becky Kajander
Linda Kapler
Elaine Kaskela
Carol Keich
Jan Kendig
Peggy Kennedy
Mary Ann Koenigsfeld
Nancy Kress
Diane Kruck
Joan Lake
Richard Larson
Mary Jane Leenstra
Melodee & Maury
  Lewin
Joyce Lewis
Susan Lipke
Froma Lippman
Sue Ludwil
Roberta Majors
Gary Manuell
Jill Marks
Debbie McDaniel
Margy McManus
Harriet Meehan
Deborah Megginson
Kathy Mellott

Gail Meyer
Mrs. John Miller
Sandi Mink
Edna Moon
Kathleen Moore
Ann Morris
Diana Nichols
Camelia Nocella
Karen Olness, M.D.
Jean Pierre
Pam Pierre
Wynann Plocher
Catherine & William
  Poulos
Kyla Reed
Phoebe Resnick
Judy Roth
Victoria Rule
John Runkle
Stanton Samenow
Sharon Schaaf
Jerry Schiller
Deidre & Ray Schipani
Cindy Schreiner
Norene & Richard
  Schulenberg
Donna Schwartz
Cynda Schwenk
Colleen Shaskin
Bonnie Silvera
Carol Sipe
Ronna Sittig
Dorothy Skelly
Deborah Smollen
Marietta Spencer
Beverly Spindler
Sheila Steiner
Pamela Stone
Wendie Stronach
Cynda Thompson
Melissa Thun
Roberta Trotta
Linda Trust
Maureen Valencia
Stephanie Wable
Gail Weiner
Sherry Weinstein
Cindie Weis
June Westphal
Felicia Wilbert
Judy Winterhalter
Karen Woods
Rhonda Wyatt DeLozier
Julie Yoder
Sandi Zimlich

Enjoy the little things, for one day you may look back and realize they were the big things . . . .

—R. Brault

CONTENTS

1. New Baby Care

2. Child Care: The Basics

3. Hygiene and Health

4. Coping with Kids at Home

5. The Challenge of Parenting

8. Child's Play

CHAPTER 1

New Baby Care

Having a baby is not unlike entering a tunnel. We can't see the end and we wonder what we've gotten ourselves into. We emerge five years later, having had less sleep than we might have wished, but thinking that it wasn't that rough after all. The difficult days become difficult to remember.

Despite the newness of everything we must do, it doesn't really take long to become old hands at baby care. Though babies don't arrive with attached instructions, they do express their needs loud and clear. And as far as our expertise is concerned, new babies don't realize that everything we do first time round is just as new for us as it is for them. WHEW!

Don't worry if you don't feel overwhelming love for your infant instantly. It often takes some time, maybe months, for real parental love to develop. Relax, and enjoy the developing bond between you and your baby.

YOUR NEW BABY AND YOU

Amid the flurry that follows the birth of a baby, it's important to remember that everyone has adjustments to make. If it's your first child, Mom and Dad are new roles to be tried out. If there are siblings in the house, their positions in the family are changed—overnight!

Along with the excitement and pride that follow a birth come stress and fatigue. You're apt to demand more of yourself than you do of those around you, but taking care of yourself adequately will make you better able to help everybody else deal with the adjustments. It's a time for spouses to be very good to each other and to put off big decisions, if possible.

* Find the "Do Not Disturb" sign from your honeymoon hotel and use it on your front door. Or make a sign: "Ssssh! Baby and Mommy are resting!"

* Disconnect the phone when you don't want to answer it, or install phone silencer switches.

* Or let modern technology help you avoid answering the phone when you don't want to. Record the details of your baby's birth on a telephone answering machine, and add a message about when is the best time to call. (You should be sleeping when your infant is.)

* Put an extension phone in your baby's room, or carry a cordless phone with you when you need to change a diaper.

* Make some part of every day special, for spouses only, whether it's a late dinner together, a walk around the block, or a five-minute noontime telephone call.

* Use paper plates and cups for now to minimize housework.

* Find some support, be it a friend who also has a new baby or an organized group.

CESAREAN DELIVERIES

If you know you'll be having a C-section, you can make some decisions before you go to the hospital. If you want the father to be present, request your doctor's permission. It may be the anesthesiologist who makes the decisions, but you'll work through your own doctor. Request minimal, local medication, if you want that. Plan to nurse the baby immediately after the anesthetic has worn off, if the baby will be breast-fed. Many prepared childbirth groups offer C-section classes.

When You Get Home

❖ Stay in bed as much as you can. Keep the baby in a bassinet or another small bed at your bedside, and keep a good supply of diapers and baby clothes handy.

❖ Get a robe that buttons all the way down the front. You'll find getting into and out of it easier than stepping in and out of one that opens only part way down.

❖ Wear a protective panty girdle to keep loose clothing from rubbing on your tender incision.

❖ Use a hair dryer to dry your incision thoroughly after a bath or shower to avoid rubbing the tender area with a towel.

❖ Put a pillow in your lap when nursing, both to support the baby and to protect your incision.

❖ Try making a playpen of your bed, if you must care for a toddler too. Keep toys and books within reach.

Caring for Tender Abdominal Muscles

❖ Use your foot as a lever to raise a toddler up to you when you are in a chair or in bed, rather than leaning down to lift a child from the floor.

❖ Use a high changing table, not a bed, to avoid bending down when you dress the baby.

❖ Avoid holding the baby in one arm while you work around the house until your muscles are stronger. Consider using a mechanical swing to save on muscle strain if the baby is fussy and wants attention.

❖ Don't vacuum for a couple of months. The movements involved are hard on abdominal muscles. (It's a good job for a father or another family member to take over.)

❖ Sit up for nursing while your baby lies facing you and off to your side. Put your arm underneath your baby and hold his or her head at your breast to keep the baby off your abdominal area.

❖ Rocking in a chair sixty or more minutes a day is reported to relieve abdominal discomfort and intestinal gas!

Cesarean Support

Cesareans/Support Education and Concern offers information about recovery from cesarean birth. For a list of support groups in your state or for a list of publications, send a business-size SASE to C/SEC, 22 Forest Road, Framingham, MA 01701, or call (508) 877-8266.

FEEDING YOUR BABY

A baby's stomach is about the size of its fist—taking in a lot of milk at one time just isn't possible. No wonder infants spend so much of their time eating!

If you're breastfeeding, the first rule is to relax. Find a quiet place away from distractions and visitors for your first feedings. And don't watch the clock. The baby doesn't. If the father feels a bit left out, remember that there are things he can do, such as changing and bathing the baby and bringing your infant to your bed for night feedings. Some parents decide to give the baby one bottle of formula a day, both to involve Dad and to let Mom get some needed sleep or a chance to get out of the house. If you use powdered infant formula, it's easy to mix up just one bottle at a time.

Support for the Nursing Mother

Contact the La Leche League International, 9616 Minneapolis Avenue, Franklin Park, IL 60131, or call 1-800-La-Leche (between 9 A.M. and 3 P.M. M–F, Central Standard Time) or (708) 455-7730 for information about the groups in your area. Women interested in the breastfeeding of infants provide information and support for one another.

Dressing Comfortably for Breastfeeding

❖ Use a front-buttoning nightgown or one with concealed slits. Bring one with you to the hospital.

❖ Wear a stretch bra that can simply be lifted up for nursing. Some women buy bras before they go to the hospital, getting a size larger (and a cup size larger) than they wore during pregnancy, but this doesn't work for everyone. Perhaps best is to buy a bra extender in a sewing notions department for the extra "give" you may need.

❖ Use a man's soft handkerchief in your bra cup to prevent leaks from coming through, use about four layers of an old knitted undershirt, or stitch together two- to three-inch circles of terry cloth. Or cut a heavy sanitary napkin or diaper to fit. (And of course there are nursing pads and other commercially available products.)

❖ Wear printed tops to make stains less visible if you leak.

❖ Unbutton front-buttoning blouses from the bottom for modest nursing. Or wear a cotton T-shirt or pullover to lift up; the baby's head will cover your bare midriff, and the T-shirt will cover your breast.

❖ Keep a cardigan sweater handy to throw over one shoulder, baby, and breast, and don't overlook the quick coverup possibilities of scarves or receiving blankets.

Comfort Setups for Nursing

❖ Protect linens and blankets when you nurse in bed by covering them with a crib-size waterproof protector.

❖ Use a big bed pillow with arms for nursing in bed.

❖ Wrap up in a big blanket, or get into a snuggle sack with the baby in the winter if you sit up to nurse at night. Or just have a sweater or robe available. Milk flows better if you're warm and cozy.

❖ Select a cushioned rocker, armchair, or sofa for nursing when you're up, one with low arms to rest your own arms on, and put a pillow under your nursing arm. If you're buying a rocker, remember that a wooden one is easier to keep clean than an upholstered one.

❖ Put the baby on a pillow on your lap; you may find that doing so puts your baby at just the right level for comfort.

Nursing Techniques

❖ Keep track of which breast you used last by transferring a safety pin from one side of your bra strap to the other. Or buy a light-weight expandable bracelet and slip it from one wrist to the other. Or use a ring that is loose enough to transfer easily from hand to hand. You may want to start on the right side each morning; you'll be able to remember how many times you've fed the baby and work out which breast you used last. Most mothers start nursing with the breast used last.

❖ Put your finger in the corner of the baby's mouth to break the suction and ease an infant off your breast when you want to stop nursing.

❖ If the baby falls asleep while nursing, change the diaper to help wake him or her when you're ready to change breasts.

❖ Wear a bright necklace of colored wooden beads or ribbons for your baby to look at while nursing.

❖ Be aware that some babies find it hard to settle down against slippery nylon or polyester. If you're wearing a shirt or top of either fabric, slip a diaper or receiving blanket between your-self and the baby.

❖ Try expressing milk in a warm shower or bath if you're engorged and the baby isn't ready to nurse. Experiment with all types of breast pumps; they don't all work for everyone.

❖ Stop an older baby who bites while nursing by pinching the baby's earlobe just hard enough to be a distraction.

Bottle-Feeding

It's understood today that a baby's food needn't be really warm, but it goes against the grain for some parents to serve up a cold bottle. A fancy electric bottle warmer isn't necessary though. Take the chill off in one of the ways suggested below, and use the time while the bottle's heating to change the baby. Test the temperature of the formula or expressed breast milk by squirting a drop or two onto your wrist; if it feels comfortably warm, it's right for the baby.

While it isn't critical for development, some parents hold their babies in one arm for one bottle feeding and the other for the next to help the infants develop good eye muscle coordination.

❖ Be very cautious if warming a bottle in your microwave. Formula or milk heats unevenly and can scald the baby's mouth. Shake it well after heating and wait thirty seconds, then shake and test it again before giving it to baby.

❖ Warm a bottle by standing it in a couple inches of water in an electric coffee maker for a few minutes; by setting it in any handy bowl, pan, mug, or wide-mouth thermos of hot water; or by running hot tap water over it. Shake the bottle occasionally to warm contents evenly.

❖ Thaw frozen breast milk in a bottle by letting it stand at room temperature until thawed, by running it under lukewarm water and gently turning (not shaking) the bottle, or by letting it sit in a pan of warm water. Don't reheat it in a microwave as this may reduce anti-infective properties.

❖ Make 2 A.M. feedings easier on parents of formula-fed babies by filling a thermos jug with warm water and keeping it in the baby's room. Mix formula instantly instead of waiting around the stove for fifteen minutes.

❖ Or take a cold (from the refrigerator) bottle to your room or the baby's when you go to bed. It will warm to room temperature by the time you need it.

❖ Have a snack ready for yourself by the baby's nighttime bottle to survive nighttime feedings. And tape your favorite TV shows to view during night feedings.

❖ Once a day, prepare all the formula you'll need for the next twenty-four hours, and store it in the refrigerator.

❖ Keep extra formula in the refrigerator to add to a too-warm bottle.

❖ If you're taking bottles somewhere and you need to keep formula or breast milk cold, put those reusable plastic ice balls you chill in the freezer in the bottles.

For an Even Flow

❖ Regulate the flow of formula by loosening the bottle collar if the flow is too slow, tightening it if the flow is too fast.

❖ Enlarge nipple holes, if necessary, by putting toothpicks in them and boiling the nipples for three minutes, or by sticking a very hot needle into the rubber a few times. If the hole is too big, toss the nipple, and start using the extras you bought!

❖ To prevent powdered formula from lumping, put the powder in first, then add water. Cap the bottle or pinch the nipple shut and shake vigorously.

❖ Eliminate all air from bottles with disposable liners by pressing up on the liner until the liquid reaches the tip of the nipple. This allows your baby to drink in an upright position. (Use leftover liners to cover recipe-type index cards!)

❖ Let your baby use bottle straws that insert into traditional nipples; formula will flow evenly no matter what position the bottle is in.

The Business of Bottles

❖ Store bottles in the refrigerator in an empty cardboard six-pack bottle holder to keep them together and safe from tipping. Or make and store formula in a sterilized glass coffee pot.

❖ A can of baby formula can be sealed with a plastic pet food lid before refrigerating.

❖ The lids from Heinz strained baby juices fit on Evenflo baby bottles.

❖ To label baby's bottles that go to day care, write the baby's name on masking tape and tape it to a wide rubber band over the bottle. It's easy to remove, and there's no tape to clean off the bottle.

❖ Open and invert your vegetable steamer basket to clean or sterilize nipples, rings, and baby bottles in boiling water. The steamer keeps all pieces under its umbrella and takes up far less space in a big pot.

❖ Boil nipples and glass bottles in water in a glass jar in the microwave oven to clean them. A teaspoonful of vinegar in the water will prevent hard water deposits in the jar.

❖ Use denture cleaner tablets to clean glass baby bottles. Let the bottles soak for a half hour according to directions; swish with a bottle brush and rinse.

❖ Rinse out empty bottles as soon as possible, or you'll find "cottage cheese" in them later. Put warm water and some dry rice in a bottle and shake to scrub out milk rings if you have no brush. To get rid of a sour-milk smell, fill bottles with warm water, add a teaspoon of baking soda, shake well, and let stand overnight.

❖ Remove juice stains by putting baking soda and warm water in the bottle and scrubbing with a bottle brush. If you don't have a bottle brush, consider using a pastry brush in its place.

❖ Or clean baby's bottle by using a dab of toothpaste with your bottle brush and just enough water to scrub it clean.

❖ Wash bottles in the dishwasher if you have one. They won't need sterilizing. To run nipples, caps, and bottle rings through the dishwasher, slip them into a zip-up mesh bag (like the ones used to wash pantyhose).

❖ Prevent bottle leaks when traveling by placing a plastic sandwich bag or square of plastic wrap across the top of the bottle and then screwing on the nipple and collar ring.

❖ Slip a lone sock over the bottle to keep little hands warm, if your baby doesn't like holding a cold bottle filled with juice or milk.

Burping

Don't worry if your baby doesn't always burp after a feeding, especially if you're breastfeeding. If he or she seems comfortable after you've given it a good try, forget it. Do be careful not to pat too hard; you may cause the baby to vomit. Some parents find it better to use a gentle upward stroke instead of patting.

❖ Put your baby on your shoulder with a diaper underneath, and gently pat the baby's back between the shoulder blades.

❖ Tie a bib around your neck if you get tired of a diaper, and switch the bib from shoulder to shoulder as you switch your baby.

❖ Lay the baby on your lap,

tummy down, with his or her head turned a little to the side.
Pat or gently rub, from the bottom up.

❖ Make a "horseshoe" with your thumb and index finger, and put
the baby's chin into it while propped on your lap, leaning
against your arm. Pat or stroke upward.

❖ Put your hand under the baby's sternum and lean the baby
toward your palm (draped with cloth or diaper), while firmly
but gently rubbing his or her back.

❖ Squeeze the baby's back gently, while the baby is on your
shoulder or in your lap, beginning at the kidney area and working slowly up to the shoulders.

PUTTING YOUR BABY TO SLEEP

Some babies sleep for long stretches of time, others catnap through the
twenty-four hours, and some seem to prefer sleeping through the day
rather than the night. Most sleep after being fed. A new baby who sleeps
through the night is the exception, not the rule, whatever your friends
and relatives may say. During the first three to six months, parents usually have to adjust their own sleeping habits to the baby's, or take shifts to
avoid exhaustion.

Inducing Sleep

Sometimes babies need a little time to cry or fuss before sleeping. You'll
soon know if the crying means something serious. Your first thought will
be for the baby's comfort. Position the baby on a side or back first. The
A.A.P., as of 1992, believes this position may reduce the risk of SIDS
(Sudden Infant Death Syndrome). While some say sleeping on the back
is best avoided to prevent newborns from gagging on milk they may spit
up, there is apparently no proven risk of aspiration.

It's not necessary or practical to try to live in a silent house. If you main-
tain a reasonable level of noise, the baby will become accustomed to it.
You may wish to play a radio softly just outside the baby's room. (But if
you find that the ring of the phone wakes the baby, turn down the ringer
volume and put a thick potholder under the phone to muffle the sound.)

> ## WATERBED WARNING!
> Never put an infant to sleep or leave a baby unattend-
> ed on an adult-size waterbed. Infants or children with
> disabilities can suffocate in the face-down position or
> by getting caught between the mattress and frame.

❖ Try to establish a sleep routine from the beginning, especially
  if you'll be traveling or expecting the baby to sleep in different
  places. Always sing the same lullaby at bedtime, or rub a special spot, perhaps the back of the head or the forehead, at sleep
  time only.

❖ Let the baby sleep upright occasionally, if comfortable, using an
  infant seat or carrying him or her in a soft fabric front carrier.

❖ Slip a warm heating pad or hot water bottle onto the sheet
  when you pick the baby up for a feeding, so the bed will be
  warm when you return him or her to it (but then take the pad
  or bottle out). Or warm a blanket in the dryer while you feed
  the baby, if that's convenient. A cold bed may have a jarring
  effect.

❖ Tape-record the sound of a running dishwasher, a running shower, or water filling the
  tub, and play it back to lull a
  child to sleep. The sound
  of running water
  simulates
  intrauterine
  sounds. Taping
  baby's own cries
  have also been
  know to work. Or
  invest in the electronic
  toy or teddy bear that duplicates intrauterine sounds.

❖ Rock and read your infant to sleep. The sound of your voice
  reading aloud a book or magazine of interest to you is still
  soothing.

❖ Put a baby down when drowsy (but awake) to learn to drift off
  to sleep without help from you.

When Your Baby Confuses Day and Night

Confusing day and night is often associated with colic. If Dad works outside the home and Mom stays home, it's logical that she bear the brunt, but she must catch up on her sleep during the day whenever the baby naps. If both parents work, trading off alternate nights helps. Try to keep the baby awake during the early evening to encourage nighttime sleep. Keep the baby slightly cool and upright in an infant seat or carrier. Talk, sing, dance, or do whatever will stimulate the baby.

❖ Adding a little instant cereal to the last evening bottle for a more substantial meal, while not scientifically substantiated, is still known to work for some.

❖ Change bathtime to just before bedtime so the baby will be relaxed.

❖ Give night feedings in dim light so the baby will realize that they're different from daytime feedings. And put your baby in the crib only at night; naps during the day can be in a carriage or playpen.

❖ Wake the baby for daytime visitors.

Making Night-Checking Easier

You won't be the first parent of a sound sleeping baby to put a small mirror under the child's nose to check for breathing, but avoid this tension-producing habit.

❖ Put a dimmer on the light switch.

❖ Keep a few strong night lights on in the baby's room.

❖ Keep a flashlight near your bed to use at night.

❖ Apply petroleum jelly or spray nonstick vegetable oil to the side rails of the crib to keep them from squeeking when they're raised or lowered. Or rub them with waxed paper.

Feeling Snug

❖ Try confining the baby gently, bundling the infant lightly in a receiving blanket. Some babies sleep better with a rather firm swaddling, reminiscent of the prebirth environment.

❖ Place the baby on his or her side. Roll up two receiving blan-

kets and put one roll down along the baby's back and neck, the
other along the stomach to support this side position. Tuck the
baby in snugly with a third blanket to hold your child in place.

❖ Position the baby in a corner of the crib or bassinet, head
touching the bumper or soft padding to provide a feeling of
security. This also allows you to move the baby from corner to
corner if the sheet gets wet or soiled.

Keeping Your Baby Cozy

❖ Test for comfort by gently touching the back of the baby's
neck. (Be sure your hand is not cold; warm it next to your
body or under hot water first if necessary.) If the baby's neck is
warm, the baby is comfortable. If it's damp, the baby may be
too warm. Arms and legs can also give a hint as to the baby's
comfort, and you can check for a pink or rosy color. Don't go
by the feeling of the baby's hands and feet. They usually feel
cool.

BEWARE OF SHEEPSKIN RUGS!

Avoid using a sheepskin rug for a very new infant—or
at least don't place the baby face-down on it until the
baby is able to lift his or her head.

❖ Use blanket sleepers of various weights, depending on the season, and skip a blanket altogether. If you're really worried
about the baby being cold, put on two sets of sleepers, but be
sure they don't bind and cut off circulation.

❖ Use a rubberized flannel lap pad over crib sheets, or spread a
diaper across the sheet, to avoid having to disturb the baby by
changing sheets after every leak and spit-up. (Rubberized flannel is available in large pieces in many fabric stores.)

❖ Cover your bassinet pad with a standard pillow case. Then just
flip it over for a dry, fresh side when needed.

❖ Make up your baby's crib sheets and pads in layers so all you
need to do is pull off a top sheet and pad to "change" sheets.

WHEN YOUR BABY CRIES

Babies cry and fuss for a variety of reasons, but you'll soon be able to translate the cry of distress. Obvious solutions are available for many cries, including cries of discomfort from being too cool or too warm, simple boredom, or relief of tension. One classic check that parents make concerns the open safety pin; another common check is for the tiny thread on the inside of a garment (or even a thread from the bassinet skirting) tangled around a baby's hand or foot and hurting. Experienced parents check carefully and clip all such threads.

Sometimes a baby just cries . . . and cries . . . and cries . . . and you know there's nothing wrong, no physical reason for it. Don't feel guilty—the baby isn't crying because you're a "bad" parent—there's nothing personal about it!

Coping with Crying

❖ Walk or dance with the baby. Try dancing to different kinds of music.

❖ Rock the baby.

❖ Bounce the baby gently in your arms or on a bed. If the baby is lying face-up, a waterbed is especially soothing.

❖ Take the baby for a ride in the carriage or the car.

❖ Put the baby in a wind-up swing. (Support the head with rolled baby blankets, towels, or one of those tiny, infant-size, head-contoured pillows that forms a halo of padding.)

❖ Turn up the music on the radio or stereo, or run the vacuum or a hair dryer.

❖ Offer the baby a "noisy" toy; shake it, rattle it.

❖ Sing or talk to the baby in a quiet, sing-song way.

❖ Carry the baby with you about the house in a soft front carrier, close to your body.

❖ Lay the baby tummy down across your lap and gently rub his or her back. You might want to swing your knees slowly back and forth.

❖ Lay the baby across a warm hot-water bottle on your lap or a bed.

❖ Massage the baby's body and limbs gently; use warmed lotion if the weather is cool. A semidark room may also help.

❖ Swaddle the baby tightly.

❖ Feed and burp the baby one more time. Or offer a little warm water. In desperation, add a tiny bit of sugar to the water or to weak camomile tea.

❖ Offer a pacifier (the molded pacifiers allow less air to pass in around the baby's mouth and are better for a colicky baby). Hold it in the baby's mouth if necessary.

❖ Or let the baby suck the top third of your little finger (turning your nail down so it won't poke the roof of the baby's mouth if he or she sucks hard).

❖ Hold the baby close and breathe slowly and calmly; the baby may feel your calmness and become quiet. While lying down, place the baby's ear over your heart.

❖ Cross the baby's arms across the chest and hold him or her down on a bed with a gentle, firm pressure.

❖ Remove yourself, and let someone else take over for awhile. If a family member is not available, consider hiring a sitter for a short period of time.

❖ If *nothing* works, put the baby in his or her bed, close the door and turn up the TV or radio. Take a shower to drown the noise and to relax yourself. Check your baby every fifteen minutes or so, for your own peace of mind.

Colic

Colic is not a disease; it can't be tested for. It's a symptom of severe cramps of the digestive tract. The baby pulls the legs up, clenches the fists, and often flushes bright red. Crying may go on for hours, often in the late afternoon and evening. Fortunately, colic rarely lasts past the third month of a child's life, but until its over, it's hard on both baby and parents.

In a breastfed baby, colic may be caused by a reaction to something in the mother's diet. Mom may try avoiding such things as strong-flavored foods and drinks that contain caffeine. Some babies are allergic to milk and other dairy products that their mothers drink or eat. A change to a soy formula that does not contain corn syrup or corn solids often helps colicky babies. Consult your doctor before you make a change.

❖ Try burping the baby before starting a feeding to prevent a bubble from being trapped at the bottom of the stomach. And burp the baby several times during a feeding.

❖ Use plastic bottle liners for a bottle-fed baby. The baby will swallow less air if the air is first squeezed out of the bag, and this will lessen abdominal discomfort.

❖ Feed the baby in as upright a position as possible. The bubble at the bottom of the baby's stomach will rise toward the top of the food and be burped easily, preventing the pain of trapped gas.

❖ Let the baby suck a peppermint candy stick; or melt a small piece of peppermint in water, and give it in a bottle. Peppermint often has a soothing effect.

❖ Or lay the baby in the crib face-up, pull the left arm and right leg away from the body gently, stretching the baby, then the right arm and left leg to relieve gas.

KEEPING YOUR BABY CLEAN

You won't be giving your baby a full bath until the umbilical cord falls off. Even then, remember that babies don't really get dirty, except for their bottoms, faces, and necks. First babies probably get bathed more than others, simply because parents have more time than they do when they have two or more children. A day without a bath is not a disgrace; skipping a day, or even several days, may be best for both you and the baby. In fact some believe that until babies begin to crawl, they only need to be bathed two or three times a week and shampooed once or twice a week. On the other hand, when you both feel the need of relaxation, a long, warm tub bath together may ease tension. You'll soon learn the best time of day for baths; immediately following a meal is best for some, but not for all.

Bath Equipment

❖ Make do at first with a plastic dishpan on the kitchen counter or bathroom vanity. You really don't need more than a few inches of warm water.

❖ Bathe the newborn in an inflatable baby tub. Or use a sculptured foam liner with the larger plastic tub.

❖ Or bathe the baby in the bathroom or kitchen sink, if the faucet is placed so that he or she is not likely to bump against it. Be careful when the baby begins to kick—his or her head may bump against the side of the sink.

❖ Use a hand-held shower hose or even your kitchen sink sprayer when bathing a baby in a baby tub. The baby will enjoy the feel of water running, and you can wash the whole body easily.

❖ Keep cotton gloves on your hands for a better grip when holding and washing your baby. Or make bath mittens from old towels.

❖ Secure a large bath towel with a diaper pin or the like around your own neck, like a bib. It will keep you dry during the bath and give you an instant wrap-up for the baby. Otherwise, wear a waterproof apron.

❖ Warm a towel near a radiator or use a hooded (in one corner) baby towel to keep your baby warm and cozy after a bath.

❖ Keep bath items in a plastic tool box carrier with a handle for easy access and ease of carrying.

Bathing Routines

❖ Keep the time babies are undressed to a minimum. When they're older they can better regulate their own body temperatures.

❖ Run the cold water last so that if the baby touches the faucet it won't be hot and burn him or her.

❖ Use even mild baby soap sparingly to preserve the baby's own protective skin oils; soap is often responsible for skin rashes. (Ivory is a strong soap; better to use Dove or Neutrogena or even a soapless soap.)

❖ Placing a baby face-down (but with face out of the water) in a frog-position with your hand supporting the chest and tummy makes it easier to handle some babies.

❖ Put a bit of cold cream or petroleum jelly on the baby's brows to channel soapy water away from the eyes.

❖ Set the plastic bottle of lotion or shampoo in the tub water with the baby and it will be warm when you're ready to use it.

❖ Cope with cradle cap by shampooing often. Use a soft bristle brush or soft toothbrush (the long handle is easy to maneuver). Treat cradle cap by smearing on baby oil or petroleum jelly at night and washing it off in the morning with a soapy washcloth. Include behind the ears too to prevent "crusties" from forming there.

❖ Put any powder you use into your hand first, away from the baby's face, so that powder in the air isn't inhaled by the baby. And for the same reason, don't let an older baby play with an open powder container. (Avoid baby powder with talc around infants.)

DIAPERING

Don't worry if you missed the Red Cross course in diapering. Parents quickly become experts and not only can but do change diapers in their sleep.

Cleaning Bottoms

Some parents like the convenience of premoistened baby wipes for cleaning babies' bottoms, but there are lots of alternatives. (P.S. If your baby wipes are drying out, store them upside down and they should stay uniformly moist in the container.)

❖ Make your own inexpensive wipes by soaking small, white paper napkins in baby oil in a shallow bowl. Store in a plastic bag or a covered container.

❖ Keep a roll of toilet paper or a box of tissues at the changing area for cleanups.

❖ Or use Handi Wipes; they rinse out easily.

❖ Or try torn-up old cloth diapers, which you can toss in the washer with the other cloth diapers.

❖ Wipe a soiled bottom clean with baby oil on a cotton ball.

❖ Try changing diapers on the bathroom vanity. Lay the baby on a towel, hold legs up, and scoot his or her bottom to the edge of the sink for hand splashing and cleaning.

❖ Color code washcloths if you use them for cleanup: one color for the bath, one for diapering.

Diapering Tricks of the Trade

❖ Keep a roll of masking tape handy to mend torn tabs on disposables and to mend plastic pants.

❖ Cover an infant boy's penis with your hand or a cloth as you expose it to avoid being squirted. Point it down when you fasten the diaper to head the stream where you want it.

Using Cloth Diapers

Because of increasing environmental concerns, more and more parents are using cloth diapers instead of disposables. To make using cloth diapers easier, you can now buy diaper wraps, which close with Velcro tabs, eliminating the need for pins. Diaper wraps come in many styles: some are waterproof covers that go over cloth diapers, and some are all one piece, with the cover already attached to the diaper. The Velcro closures do, however, collect lint in the washer and dryer. Periodically use a pin or stiff toothbrush to clean the lint out of these closures, or brush the rough tabs against each other. For diapers without built-in closures, diaper clips are available that work like tiny clamps. If you prefer to stick with or need to use diaper pins, keep the following in mind:

* Always use diaper pins with plastic covered ends, never ordinary safety pins.

* Place your fingers between the baby's skin and the diaper to prevent sticking him or her with a pin.

* Snap a wrist pincushion around the top rung of the crib or dressing table as a diaper pin holder when the baby is tiny. It's not a safe procedure when a child is old enough to reach for it. Or stick pins in a thick potholder or hang closed pins on a cup hook screwed into the wall.

* Stick pins in a bar of soap with the paper wrapping left on to contain flakes, to make them slide through cloth easily. Or stick them in a decorative candle for attractive storage.

* Run pins through a strand of your hair or across the top of your head to make them go through cloth easily.

* Attach a few diaper pins to your key chain so that you'll always have extras handy when you're away from home.

* Don't hold pins in your mouth—babies are great imitators!

Preventing Diaper Rash

Experienced parents may smile a bit at the thought of "preventing" diaper rash. It seems that almost every baby has it to some degree at one time or another.

* Give the baby warm, soapy baths with mild soap. Bathe bottoms even when not giving a full bath—make sure to clean gently in sensitive areas.

❖ Don't use fabric softener with every diaper wash. Babies are often sensitive to softener buildup (and overuse makes diapers less absorbent).

❖ Don't use plastic or rubber pants that don't "breathe." They hold moisture in, preventing evaporation. Change the baby often to avoid diaper rash.

❖ Smooth on solid vegetable shortening; it's cheaper than commercial preparations and usually works as well. Petroleum jelly, at about the same cost, is also good. (Storing it in a plastic squeeze bottle makes it easier to handle.)

❖ Keep a rubber spatula on your changing table to apply petroleum jelly or another moisture barrier to your child's bottom. It keeps your hands clean and avoids problems with strips on disposables not sticking. Or use inexpensive wedge-shaped make-up sponges.

❖ Try applying zinc oxide or a paste of cornstarch and water. (Current opinion is mixed as to the advisability of using cornstarch alone, however.)

Treating Diaper Rash

Once the baby has diaper rash, you try one thing . . . and then another. Many doctors oppose "greasing" a baby with oils and lotions, and experienced parents don't use any solutions or ointments too thickly—"more is better" doesn't apply here.

❖ Consider disposables if you've been using cloth diapers and vice versa. The change often helps.

❖ Let the baby stay naked or at least bare-bottomed as often as possible—a light case of diaper rash may be air- or sun-cured quickly.

❖ Expose the baby's bottom to the air while he or she naps. Just place a folded diaper underneath your baby to protect the bedding.

❖ Dry the baby's bottom between diaper changes with a hair dryer set at "warm" and held at least six inches from the skin.

❖ Avoid premoistened baby wipes that contain alcohol. They can be too drying.

❖ Fill a spray bottle with a half tablespoon of baking soda dissolved in 16 ounces of water. Vigorously spray your child's bottom to remove stool and urine, then gently wipe away any remaining soilage. Blot the skin dry, and apply ointment or powder before fastening on a new diaper.

❖ You may find an over-the-counter preparation that works. If serious diaper rash persists, check with your doctor for a prescription.

Making the Dressing Area Convenient

You may find it practical to set up a "satellite" dressing area to save steps. Keep it stocked with diapers, clothing, and duplicates of other essential items. Or keep baby supplies in a clean plastic carry-all and take it about the house with you.

❖ Use decorative kitchen cannisters to hold baby items near the changing table.

❖ Use the top of a dresser for a changing table. Cut an old belt in half and staple the ends to the top of the dresser to make a safety belt for the baby. Line the drawers with wrapping paper from your baby shower gifts to make them attractive.

❖ Cover your changing table pad with a pillowcase, which can be removed and laundered easily.

❖ Or sew two bath towels together to cover your changing pad. Make two or three of them so it's easy to toss one in the laundry as necessary.

❖ Hang a shelf above the changing table to hold necessities and to keep them up out of the reach of toddlers.

❖ Or make or buy a wall hanging (about two feet square) with pockets for small articles. It can be hung with curtain rods on the top and bottom. A shoe bag also works well.

❖ Keep a thermos of warm water near the changing table at night for quick cleanups. You'll avoid stumbling around in the dark and running the water for what seems hours to get the right temperature.

❖ Save time by folding traditional diapers only as you need them. Keep a laundry basket of clean, unfolded diapers near the dressing area.

❖ Keep two diaper pails at the dressing area: one for soiled diapers (smallish and, if you use cloth diapers, half filled with water to which borax has been added so that it won't get smelly) and the other for wet or soiled clothing that will later be transferred to the laundry.

❖ Cut down on cleaning chores by using plastic liners inside the diaper pail.

Another Use for . . . Baby Wipes

❖ Mom, use to wipe tender episiotomy sutures.
❖ Wipe down bathroom surfaces for a quick clean-up.
❖ Clean scrapes and bruises and soothe sunburn.
❖ Take off eye makeup.
❖ Blot up spills and remove some stains.
❖ Use as toilet paper for your toilet-training toddler.
❖ Clean hands after pumping gas.

BABY LAUNDRY

It's unbelievable to new parents that one tiny person can generate so much laundry—and it's always a surprise, even to those who have gone through it more than once. If you use cloth diapers, you want them not only clean but also germ-free, to help prevent diaper rash.

Cloth Diapers

❖ Rinse out diapers, even those that are only wet, before putting them in the diaper pail. Empty soiled diapers in the toilet.

❖ Sprinkle a little baking soda in the diaper pail to keep diapers from souring.

❖ Soak diapers overnight in the washing machine with soap and a commercial soaking solution. Run them through the regular cycle the next day, then run once more without soap for a good rinse.

❖ Or soak in a plastic bag in the diaper pail filled with water and about a cup of borax.

❖ Add a handful of baking soda to the next-to-last rinse to keep the diapers soft and fresh smelling. Fabric softener is expensive and may cause skin irritation.

❖   Or try another old-fashioned diaper softener and whitener—
    vinegar. A cupful in the second rinse gets rid of soap and helps
    prevent diaper rash.

❖   Instead of bleach, use $^1/_4$ cup ammonia in the diaper pail or
    laundry. It works great and doesn't eat up diapers like bleach
    does.

❖   Use an inch or so of kitty litter or baking soda in the bottom of
    your baby's diaper pail to absorb the odors of disposable dia-
    pers. Change once a week to keep it fresh.

❖   Rub a little baby oil into plastic pants that are becoming dry
    and brittle. Or try putting the oil into the rinse water.

Stained Clothes

❖   Soak stained clothes (or mildewed hand-me-downs) in hot
    water with a half-cup each of vinegar and laundry soap.

❖   Or soak clothes overnight in hot water with a cup each of
    laundry detergent, bleach, and dishwasher detergent. Finish
    the wash cycle in the morning, run the clothes through a regu-
    lar warm wash cycle, and give them an extra rinse to be sure all
    chemicals are out of the fabric.

❖   Dab at soured dribbles on the baby's clothes with a moistened
    cloth dipped in baking soda.

❖   Carry a stain remover stick in a diaper bag (or keep one on
    hand near your changing area) to apply to spots before they
    set.

❖   Remove baby formula from color-fast clothing by dipping a
    toothbrush in Murphy's Oil Soap and scrubbing the stain out.

❖   Remove a formula stain from baby's white clothing by wetting
    the stain and sprinkling it with scouring powder that contains
    bleach or baking soda. Brush it out with a toothbrush.

❖   Put baby's socks into a mesh bag before washing so none get
    lost.

Ready-to-Go Baby Bag

Keep a prepacked bag to grab as you go out the door with the baby. Stock it with diapers, an extra set of clothes, wipes, a light blanket, and plastic bags (those that come in a roll are handy—always there!). A two-foot square of plastic or washable vinyl wallpaper can be put down anywhere for quick changes. Save the free samples of baby products you receive in the hospital for your traveling bag, and keep the containers to refill with the contents of larger sizes. Keep a clean bottle set in the bag with dry formula in it (use the bottle for water if you're breastfeeding). You might also include a pillowcase to pop a blanket-wrapped baby into for snug warmth in winter and to keep a blanket from shedding on your clothes. And don't forget to restock your bag as soon as you return home from your outing. Leave room for your wallet and a hairbrush and you won't need to carry a purse. Or carry a fanny pack for your personal items.

A STIMULATING ENVIRONMENT

Gradually, your whole house will become baby- and child-oriented, but the baby's own room will probably be the one most interesting to him or her. Remember that newborns can focus their eyes only on objects 7 to 12 inches away. By three months of age, a baby can focus well on more distant objects.

Stimulating Your Baby

Use as much color in the baby's room as you can, in paint, curtains, and wall hangings. Buy or make a bright-colored patchwork quilt; use printed sheets on the crib (colorful double sheets folded in half work well and can be used later on a big bed). Remember that infants see the colors red and yellow best and they love faces, especially those with prominent eyes. Cheer yourself up and stimulate your baby by wearing bright, patterned clothes yourself. Sew a colorful fabric cover for a vinyl-covered crib bumper, both

to protect the vinyl, which tears easily, and to make it more attractive.

❖ Decorate a wall with a montage of baby congratulation cards or frame some cards to hang separately. Or hang some cute plastic placemats.

❖ Fasten bright decals on the insides of the crib, bassinet, or carriage. Make sure you remove them before your baby is old enough to remove them and eat them.

❖ Cut out pictures of smiling babies. Babies seem to know and love these faces.

❖ Put a colorful poster, kite, or piece of wallpaper on the ceiling above the dressing table. Or hang an inflated punch ball balloon.

❖ Place a small cork board over the dressing table to display bright drawings for the baby made by an older sibling.

❖ Hang your infant's "progress calendar" near your changing area so you'll remember to note that day's progress or new activity.

❖ Keep a music box in the baby's room to appeal to the sense of sound, or hang wind chimes near a window that will be open in warm weather.

❖ Put your baby's infant seat on the floor, where it's possible to see more. And put a mirror tile on the wall nearby—fun for your infant now and for your crawling child later!

❖ Hang some of the baby's toys and rattles on the crib with snap-on plastic shower curtain hooks. They're bright and strong; they keep toys in view and off the floor.

❖ Cut off the band of a bright colored sock or one with color bands to place on an infant's wrist. As baby's hands move, the colorful wristband will capture his or her attention.

❖ Attach small stuffed animals to the crib bumper with pieces of Velcro.

❖ Or decorate with brightly colored potholders. They're safe and can eventually be used in the kitchen.

❖ Decorate your baby's high chair with a colorful picture or decal. Cover it with two coats of polyethylene to make it permanent.

❖ A wadded ball of transparent tape in the hands of a baby has a long play value for texture and sound. Be sure the ball is larger than the baby's mouth so that the baby can't swallow it or chew pieces off.

❖ Keep a baby occupied for a long time in a high chair by smearing a thin layer of peanut butter and milk on the baby's hands.

Social Life with Your Baby

Remember to serve only finger foods that can be eaten with one hand when you have a party with other parents and their new babies. Everyone will have a baby on one arm!

SAVING MONEY ON EQUIPMENT

It's not necessary for parents to buy every available piece of equipment for babies; there are many workable substitutes, especially for the first few months of an infant's life when changes take place so quickly.

❖ Use a padded laundry basket or a travel crib for a comfortable, portable in-house bed.

❖ Carry the baby's bathtub for sleeping away from home, or pad a deep dresser drawer for the baby to sleep in when you're visiting.

❖ Let a carriage serve as an infant bed. It can be gently rocked, as a crib can't.

❖ Substitute a small inflatable plastic wading pool for a playpen for a child who's not yet actively crawling.

❖ Make a bathtub or outdoor toy storage container out of a large plastic plant pot. It allows for good drainage!

❖ Use a carpet remnant to fit the floor of your child's playpen. It keeps the baby warmer, and it's easy to remove for cleaning.

YOUR BABY'S SIBLINGS

If there is an older child in your family, he or she will no doubt be excited at the prospect of a new baby. Before the baby is born, you'll want to explain how it's in Mommy's uterus where the older child once was, and let the child feel the baby's movements. And you'll want to talk about the baby as it will be after birth: sleeping, crying, eating, and taking a lot of Mommy and Daddy's time. Be sure your older child doesn't expect an instant playmate!

Preparing the Older Sibling

❖ Move the older child up a step or two before the baby arrives—to a big bed from a crib, to another bedroom, to nursery school for a day or two a week—so that these changes won't be seen as rejections after the baby arrives.

❖ Babysit another baby a few times to let your child see how things will be. You'll get a little practice, and the visiting baby's parents will owe you.

❖ Take your child to the hospital, have lunch in the coffee shop, and let the child help pick out a present for the baby and one for himself or herself. If possible, visit the nursery where the baby will be. This will be your chance to talk to your child about what will be happening while you're in the hospital. And the hospital will become a known quantity.

❖ Take your child with you to a prenatal checkup to hear the baby's heartbeat if your doctor's agreeable. Have the doctor answer any questions your child may have.

❖ Shop together for a new outfit for the baby.

❖ Have your child talk to the baby using your navel as the microphone.

❖ Involve Daddy actively. If he will be in charge of the older child at home, have him let the child know how happy he'll be when they spend that special time together.

❖ And don't start any of this too early! The nine months may seem to go slowly for you, but for a child they are an eternity.

While You're Gone

❖ Tape-record some stories for your child to listen to while you're in the hospital.

❖ Leave a picture of yourself in your child's room.

❖ Prepare some little gifts to be handed out each day while you're gone.

❖ Send home little gifts from the hospital: flexible straws, packets of jelly, plastic cups.

❖ Ask your older child to take care of something special for you while you're in the hospital—perhaps a scarf or piece of jewelry.

❖ Put a picture of your older child in your baby's hospital bassinet so the baby can "get to know" the big brother or sister.

❖ Call your child frequently from the hospital, especially if children are not allowed to visit on the maternity floor.

❖ Let your child bring a small treat such as a granola bar or sucker (wrapped with a pink or blue ribbon) to pass out to each classmate to announce the birth.

❖ Don't walk into your home carrying the baby on your return, if possible. Let someone else hold the baby so you can devote a few minutes to your reunion with the older child.

Helping Siblings Deal with Jealousy

It's important to understand that for your older child the trauma of a rival is very real. Jealousy may not appear until the baby is older and develops a real personality, but you should be prepared for it. You may want to allow any temporary regression of the older child to run its course with as little notice and comment as possible, while praising any particular grown-up behavior displayed. Don't expect the child to love the baby instantly. Make it 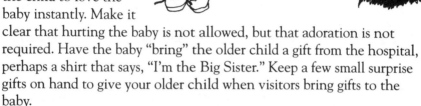 clear that hurting the baby is not allowed, but that adoration is not required. Have the baby "bring" the older child a gift from the hospital, perhaps a shirt that says, "I'm the Big Sister." Keep a few small surprise gifts on hand to give your older child when visitors bring gifts to the baby.

❖ Plan ten to fifteen minutes (minimum) a day for one-on-one time alone with your older child that he or she can count on and perhaps even plan.

❖ Express your own occasional annoyance with the baby's demands to your older child, but not so often that the big brother or sister gets the idea that the new sibling is a permanent nuisance. Express your joy, too.

❖ Put a stool next to the baby's dressing table so that your older child can watch changing and dressing routines.

❖ Have a basket of special toys that come out when you're feeding the baby; or watch a videotape together.

❖ Let the child help as much as possible with "our baby," holding, singing, or talking to the baby and running errands around the house for you. Show your appreciation for the help.

❖ Set the baby's crib mattress at the lowest point so that an older child won't be able to try to pick the baby up—even if it's harder on your back.

❖ "Stall" visitors who come to see the baby so that the older child can be the center of attention for a few minutes. Show pictures of the child as well as of the baby. Then let the child help you show off the baby.

❖ Expect and allow some regression on the older child's part. Maybe the older child will now like foods served in a baby-food jar and will enjoy playing with the baby's toys.

❖ Give the older child new privileges: a later bedtime, increased spending money or allowance, special things to do with a parent.

❖ Teach the older child that by smiling often at the baby, he or she will soon "teach" the baby to smile.

The Other Kind of "Sibling"

To help the family dog or cat adjust to the new baby, bring home one of the baby's diapers or blankets the day before the baby is brought home, and give it to the pet to play with and sniff. The baby's odor will then be a familiar one. You can "pet proof" the baby's room by putting a gate across the door or by installing a screen door. You'll still be able to see into the room and pets will be kept out.

WELL-CHECKUP VISITS

❖ Keep a notepad in a convenient place in your home to make running notes of questions you want to ask at the baby's check-ups. Note your baby's "history," including sleeping, crying, and eating patterns, elimination habits, and such.

❖ Don't be afraid to ask anything. A "foolish" question is better than a mistake.

❖ Make written notes of any verbal instructions the doctor or pediatric nurse practitioner gives you; what seems perfectly clear in the office may become less so by the time you get home.

❖ Save yourself trouble by having the baby wear a disposable diaper for a doctor visit even if you normally use cloth ones. You won't have to take a wet or soiled diaper home. And take masking tape with you so you can reuse the diaper if it's still dry.

Reasons to Call the Doctor

❖ The first occurrence of any illness new to the baby, even a cold.

❖ Diarrhea, when bowel movements are more watery and more frequent than usual.

❖ Blood-tinged urine or bowel movements.

❖ Poor feeding, when the baby stops the usual vigorous sucking during feedings.

❖ Unusual crying that continues, or a hoarse, husky cry.

❖ A significant change in the baby's color, breathing, behavior, or activity.

❖ A rectal temperature of 101° F or higher.

❖ A listless, inactive attitude if the baby is usually active and alert; or drowsiness at an unusual time, lasting a long time.

❖ Convulsions, "fits," or spells during which the child stiffens or twitches uncontrollably.

❖ Draining ears or ear pain, shown by constant turning of the head, pulling at the ear, or crying when coughing.

❖ Forceful or projectile vomiting instead of the usual spitting up or cheesing.

❖ A serious-looking rash that covers a large part of the baby's body and is unfamiliar to you.

❖ Redness of or discharge from the baby's eyes.

❖ Any injury from which the pain or disability doesn't disappear within fifteen minutes.

WORKING MOMS

Moms who work outside the home and plan to return to the workplace after their baby is born must start planning child care during their pregnancy as well as postpartum help. It's important to have contingency plans because you will certaintly need them. As it is said, "The best laid plans. . . ." Be flexible, and keep your sense of humor. No one manages work and family without hitches. Remember, returning to work involves two separate and equally important parts: leaving your child, and reentry as a productive employee who has been out of the mainstream for awhile.

Prior to Your Return

❖ Phone your office occasionally before returning and have important memos sent to you to make reentry easier.

❖ Set up a meeting with your boss before you actually go back to work. You can talk about what you'll be doing upon your return and get an idea of how you'll want to organize your business day.

❖ Select a pediatrician convenient to either your daycare facility or your home. Let your travel time and work hours determine your choice of location.

❖ Start bringing your child to the daycare provider on a part-time basis for a week or two before you go back to work. This will help you adjust to having to leave your child, and it will help your child adjust to being left. It will also give you time to attend to personal errands you may not have time for once you begin working.

First Days Back at Work

❖ Plan a light schedule for your first day back on the job, or consider a part-time reentry schedule.

❖ Grieving is sometimes a part of what you feel when you face leaving your child and returning to work. This feeling will pass once you realize that those smiles and first steps are still waiting for you at the end of your work day.

❖ Call your sitter as often as it makes you comfortable in the beginning.

❖ Don't worry if you feel a bit of competition with your child's caretaker. That's normal.

CHAPTER TWO

Child Care: The Basics

The routines of feeding, clothing, and getting your child to sleep move slowly from things you do for them to things you help them do themselves. While it often seems easier to do it all yourself, you'll want to encourage as much self-help as possible.

FEEDING

If you worry about "getting" the baby to eat, don't. It's not really possible. You can control the quality and variety that you offer, but the baby should control the quantity that's taken in. Be aware that children's appetites usually decrease dramatically at about one year of age because their growth slows. And as for your child's attitudes, respect strong food dislikes. Your job is to provide preferred, nutritious foods. Your child should determine the amounts he or she wants to eat.

Feeding the Baby

❖ Warm baby food in an egg poacher, using the compartments for different foods.

❖ Use paper muffin cups or coffee filters for some appropriate baby foods and save on dishwashing.

❖ Puree foods in a blender, food mill, or food processor (if it's all you have on hand) in quantity and freeze them in ice cube trays (or in "plops" on cookie sheets), then transfer to plastic bags. Cubes thaw quickly and are easy to take along for meals away from home.

❖ Feed a young child a banana right out of the peel with a spoon, one bite at a time. The rest of the banana will stay fresh.

❖ Make your own baby oatmeal by placing rolled oats in your blender or food processor and cooking this fine flour-like cereal with water or milk until it's the right consistency.

❖ Serve sugared cereals as an after-dinner treat.

❖ Add a little liquid to soft-cooked meats to make them easier to grind in a baby-food grinder. In the same grinder, you can puree most of your own table foods, unseasoned, for your baby.

❖ Use a long-handled spoon that fits the baby's mouth. Plastic-coated spoons feel good on tender gums.

❖ Keep the baby from sliding down in a high chair by putting a rubber sink mat or stick-on, nonslip bathtub daisies or strips on the seat.

❖ Use a fabric high chair insert that attaches to the back of the chair and then ties around your child. It helps a very young child sit up while holding him or her securely in place. It's good for travel, too, as it can turn many a standard high back chair into a high chair.

When There's No High Chair

To "trap" a small child for feeding (when a high chair's not available or the child is too small for one) and still provide comfort: cross your left leg over your right knee at the ankle, forming a triangle. (Reverse the position if you are left-handed.) Set the child in the triangle. A child can't get out, can't squirm. A bonus is that you can feed the child between bites of your own meal.

Bibs

❖ Try using a molded plastic bib with a "lip"; it provides a good catchall. Or try to find a bib with cap sleeves to keep the baby's clothes clean. If the bib isn't waterproof on at least one side, save it for "drool and dribble."

❖ For an inexpensive, durable, easy-to-clean bib, use a kitchen towel that comes with crocheted, snap handles that hang from the refrigerator to go around baby's neck.

❖ Make instant disposable bibs from plastic grocery bags that have handles. Slit the back and cut the bottom off the bag. Have children slip arms through the handles.

❖ Try using an apron or adult T-shirt (you can always find some cheap ones at garage sales) instead of a bib to protect the child's clothes from stains.

❖ To make terry-cloth bibs waterproof, sew scratchy vinyl bibs to the backs. Your baby's chin will be protected by the soft terry cloth.

❖ Pin a fabric bib to your baby's clothes for better coverage.

❖ Tuck a double thickness of facial or toilet tissue under the neckline of the bib to keep drools from running down the baby's neck.

❖ Try a colorful bandana for a child who's a "bib-resister." The folds may catch some of the spills.

❖ Use clip clothespins to attach a dishtowel or napkin to clothes. Older children, in particular,will keep their clothes clean but won't feel like they are wearing a bib.

Gnaw-ons for Teethers

Most children are bothered to some extent by teething, though discomfort varies widely. All babies begin to drool at about three months. This is not a sign of teething. Nor is fever a normal part of this process. Pressure seems to soothe gums and help teeth erupt more efficiently. Consider the following gnaw-ons:

❖ A cold or frozen bagel. (Beware of chunks that a child might gum or bite off and choke on.)

❖ A chilled navel orange, cut into sections. Or unpeeled chunks of apple or other fruits. (Caution, as above.)

❖ A cold or frozen carrot or stringless cold celery. (Caution, as above.)

❖ A frozen banana, or a lengthwise-cut piece of one. (Caution, as above.)

❖ The core of a fresh pineapple, cut into quarters. The core is not as strong-tasting as the rest of the fruit, but it still may be a bit too acid for some children.

❖ Frozen teething rings; chilled pacifiers.

❖ A dampened washcloth or soft potholder, frozen and stored in a plastic bag.

❖ An ice cube, tied into a washcloth with a short, secured string.

❖ A toothbrush.

❖ A clean rubber canning ring.

❖ A new, clean rubber ring from the puppy department of your supermarket.

❖ Or a dog biscuit. Really! They're not harmful in any way. (Caution, as above.)

Do-It-Yourself Eaters

Self-feeding is messy, and it often takes a child a long time to eat even a small meal, but you should encourage it anyway. Don't panic if your child prefers fingers to spoons; they're faster, and the feeling of food is as important to a child as its color and flavor. The finer points of etiquette can be picked up later. Just make things as easy as possible for the child (and yourself), and let him or her go to it!

❖ Put a rubber suction soap holder on the tray to keep the plate or bowl from slipping and to free both the baby's hands for eating. Or use a weighted plastic pet bowl. It's heavy (and hard to toss or turn over) and it's unbreakable!

❖ Pile the baby's food right on the high-chair tray at first, and avoid the problem of the thrown plate. (Cut a plastic place mat to fit the shape of your high-chair tray so it makes the tray easier to clean.)

❖ Give the baby a spoon in each hand and use one yourself. The baby will imitate you. Demitasse or small sugar spoons and hors d'oeuvres forks (not too sharp!) are easy for babies to eat from. And for a real beginner, consider a wooden tongue depresser as a scoop for food.

❖ Give a child who insists on eating from a big plate a plastic one with a raised rim. Many have divided sections.

❖ Give a butter spreader or plastic picnic knife to a child who wants all the tools for eating that grownups have.

❖ Mashed potatoes is a good first food for self-servers as it adheres to utensils.

❖ Rinse large-curd cottage cheese in a colander with running water. The remaining large pieces make a perfect finger food.

❖ Roll banana slices in graham cracker crumbs or toasted wheat germ to make them less slippery to pick up.

❖ Mix yogurt or applesauce instead of milk with dry cereal for a manageable solid when a child hasn't yet mastered handling a spoon. Or make hot cereal very pasty so it stays on the spoon.

❖ Serving soup? Give your child a straw to sip cooled soup and a spoon to eat the veggies with. It minimizes splatters.

❖ Allow extra time to feed a self-feeder.

❖ Feed a self-feeder just prior to bathtime!

Do-It-Yourself Drinkers

If you are bottle-feeding your child, slip a brightly colored sock or a terry sport wristband over the bottle to make it easier for the baby to hold. Slipping a few rubber bands or attaching a bathtub appliqué around the bottle will serve the same purpose. When weaning a child to a cup, begin by reducing bottle feedings and ask your child to help you deliver bottles to someone else's baby who needs them. Or take the nipple off the bottle and let the baby drink from the lip of the bottle. You may also want to cut the nipple off the bottle and tell the baby the bottle is "broken." He or she will soon be convinced.

❖ Let a toddler learn to drink from a cup in the bathtub.

❖ A drinking glass is easier for little hands to hold if you use the tips listed on the previous page for bottles that allow the child to get a good grip.

❖ When young children no longer want to drink from a baby cup or "tippy cup," give them commuter cups to use. They hold more and spill less. And they make a child feel grown-up.

❖ Fill glasses only about a third full (until your child is more skilled) to prevent waste if they're spilled.

❖ Or let the child drink from a plastic medicine or eyewash cup. They're easier to hold and won't soak him or her if they're spilled. A variation: three-ounce paper cups.

❖ Draw or tape a circle on the high-chair tray to show your child where the cup goes. (Not too close to the edge!)

❖ Let your child use a bright-colored straw, or several of them, for drinking from a glass, cup, or can. Cut straws off two inches above the top so the child won't tip the drink.

❖ Turn the tab on a can of pop around so it is over the opening, and it will help hold a straw in place.

❖ Use a clean, plastic pancake syrup bottle as a drinking container for a child. The pop-up top prevents spills. It's also good for car travel.

❖ Use the lightweight plastic bottles that bicyclers use as spill-proof containers for kids.

❖ Turn the little plastic bear in which honey is packaged into a spill-proof drinking container. Rinse it thoroughly, and cut the upper end of a cap to the diameter of a drinking straw. (Tie a bow around its neck for a great party favor!)

❖ Use an empty Dannon-style yogurt cup for a non-spill container for kids. Put a hole in the center of the lid the size of a straw.

❖ Avoid wasting paper cups or washing excess dishes by assigning each person a specific mug. When the child is finished, have him or her rinse it in hot water and turn it upside down on the dish drainer or a terry towel. When the child needs a cup again, he or she can just reach to the countertop.

Easy Eating

❖ Quickly cool many foods that are too hot for a toddler by dropping an ice cube into them.

❖ Serve bran muffins slightly frozen. They're nutritious and produce fewer crumbs.

❖ Puree meat or vegetables a baby won't eat, and use them as sandwich spreads; finger foods often go down more easily than those which must be eaten with a spoon.

❖ Or mash leftovers, mix them with an egg, and cook like pancakes, or bake them in muffin tins.

❖ Thicken soup for less liquidy spills when children are eating by adding instant potatoes a little at a time when cooking.

❖ Substitute vanilla ice cream when you're out of milk. (It works well with waffles and hot cereal.)

❖ Give your little one grated cheese. It's the perfect size for little fingers, and it's ready to serve when they can't wait.

For Older Tots

❖ Let your child choose his or her breakfast by dividing favorite dry cereals into individual servings and placing them somewhere that is easily accessible to the child. Alternate with individual packets of instant oatmeal and cream of wheat. Convenient and nutritious.

❖ To help your child in the morning, put out a lidded bowl of cereal, and put glasses of milk and juice in the refrigerator. When the child gets up, all he or she has to do is pour the milk over the cereal.

❖ Help teach your child to use chopsticks by making them easier to hold: fold a piece of paper between the two chopsticks at one end, then wind a rubber band around them to secure them at the top.

❖ Require your child to eat the same number of bites of vegetables as his or her age. (This rule seems to balance age differences, as a younger child can feel special for having to eat less, and an older child gains a certain status for the number of vegetables eaten.)

❖ Make a list of "yes" foods that children can eat whenever

they're hungry—without asking you. For example: bananas, apples, carrots, water chestnuts, raisins (frozen raisins are a fun treat), and rice cakes.

❖ When you need to serve several pointed-bottom cones at once, stand them in a block of styrofoam in your freezer.

Creative "Containers"

❖ Let a hungry child have a paper bag of small goodies (small edibles he or she can pull from the bag to feel and eat) while you prepare the meal.

❖ Give your child cereal or soup in a plastic cup or mug with a handle to grasp. The remaining milk or broth can be drunk instead of spooned out.

❖ Use a molded ice cube tray to chill Jell-O Jigglers (aka "Knox Blox") for ready-to-eat squares.

❖ Fill the compartments of a muffin tin with different finger foods such as cheese cubes, strips of cold meat, crackers, raw vegetables, or fruit. It's called a "potpourri lunch."

❖ Serve an occasional meal on a doll plate, an aluminum pie plate, or a new Frisbee—just for fun.

❖ Fill an ice cream cone with tuna or egg salad, cottage cheese, or yogurt for easy eating. It's a good on-the-run lunch for an older child, too.

❖ Make children's sandwiches using hot-dog buns. They are easier for kids to hold. And serve Sloppy Joes in unsliced burger buns. Slice off the "caps," dig out excess bread, fill, and recap.

❖ Use wooden popsicle sticks to serve anything from a section of apple to a hot dog.

❖ Use refrigerator biscuits to make peanut butter and jelly sandwiches for little hands.

❖ For a change of pace, wrap a flour tortilla around a hot dog. Try adding grated cheese and microwaving for 30 seconds. Or add guacamole, sour cream, or salsa for a Mexican flavor.

❖ Fill flat-bottom ice cream cones half full with your favorite cake mix. Bake on a cookie sheet at 350° for 20 minutes. Cool and frost, and top with a maraschino cherry. For a birthday, add a scoop of ice cream on top of the baked cupcake. (In a microwave you can cook two cones at a time in 45 seconds.)

Creative Design

❖ Let a preschooler make a "dangerous dinner." It's constructed with toothpicks held together with pieces of meat, chunks of cheese and vegetables, dried fruits, or anything good. When it's "built," it's ready to eat.

❖ Slit hot dogs lengthwise one to three times so they're in narrow strips before serving. Small circular pieces or bites can block a child's air passage if not well chewed.

❖ When pieces of apple are too slippery for a child to hold, peel and core a whole apple and have the child hold on to it by slipping a thumb or finger through the center.

❖ Arrange berries or pieces of fruit in a design on cooked cereal so your child will eat it.

❖ Use a pizza cutter or a canape cutter to cut spaghetti or pancakes into bite-size pieces for your child. It's also a handy tool for trimming off bread crusts for those who won't eat them and for cutting popsicles in half. You may want to enhance feelings of independence by letting your child cut his or her own food with the pizza cutter.

❖ Use a ready-made refrigerated pie crust that can be unfolded when the kids want to make cookies and you don't have time. Pull out the cookie cutters and sprinkle the dough with sugar sprinkles or cinnammon sugar, and all you have to do is bake the cookies.

❖ Hide food treats in the cabinet in an empty oatmeal container. Kids never think to look there.

❖ Use the crisper bins of the refrigerator for your child's favorite lunch foods. Give the child the responsibility to pack lunch with the items found in this bin to cut down on time spent preparing lunches.

Strategies for Food Jags and Picky Eaters

Don't panic. The number of calories and amounts of food that authorities recommend for health and growth is an average. Some people burn more calories, others less. Learn substitutions. Serve smaller portions. Offer healthy snacks. Don't keep sweets around. Find "good" fast foods.

While most are high in salt, fat, and calories, some, such as pizza, do have a higher nutritional value. Avoid fighting about food. Make up the difference with vitamins. Give up what you can't control.

- Let your child choose one cereal (usually sugared), and you choose another (unsweetened). Mix the two and serve for breakfast as a compromise.

- Or serve inexpensive, low-sugar cereals topped with just a bit of any of the following to give them more interest while actually adding very little extra sugar: coconut, candy sprinkles, one or two gummy bears, chocolate drink mix, a few chocolate chips, or a little premixed sugar and cinnamon.

- One way to get children to eat is to have them drop their food (chicken, tuna, etc.) into an electric food chopper and allow them to press the button. They feel that they've helped prepare it and will usually eat it.

- Add a few drops of vanilla extract to milk for a child who won't drink milk. Serve it with a bright colored straw and the child will enjoy it just like a milk shake.

- Don't assume food rejected three weeks ago will be rejected now.

- Put sugar in an aluminum shaker for a child to use when adding sugar to cereals. It eliminates spills and avoids the problem of too much sugar in one spot . . . as well as making it easier to cut back on sugar use.

- Cut food with a cookie cutter and decorate it with faces to encourage fussy food fanatics.

- Don't feed kids until they're hungry. It may mean that their mealtimes are different from yours. Consider a snack a meal and make it nutritious.

- Add condiments to encourage eating nutritious foods. Put ketchup on peas, ranch dressing on vegetables.

❖   Some tots eat better when roaming. Put a gate on the doorway to the kitchen and realize that this stage too shall pass.

Treat Tricks

❖   To avoid messy cleanups, insert your child's popsicle in a disposable cup that you have trimmed to about half its original size. Make a slit for the stick in the bottom of the cup, and the cup catches the drips. Coffee filters work well here, too.

❖   Fill balloons with whatever juice you want. Put a popsicle stick in the hole and tie. When frozen, cut away the balloon for a giant popsicle!

❖   Use transparent tape across the cup top to hold popsicle sticks upright when making frozen flavored ice in paper cups.

❖   For a birthday treat, insert popsicle sticks into cookies before baking to make "cookie pops." Frosting is optional.

❖   Give a wooden popsicle stick to a child to frost cupcakes. It's safe to lick when the job is done.

❖   Put a malted milk ball or marshmallow in the bottom of the cone when serving ice cream cones to help minimize leaks. A banana slice is a more nutritious variation.

❖   After the soda in bottles goes flat and no one wants to drink it, pour it into an ice cube tray for "tasty pops."

❖   Freeze leftover candy from winter holidays and Halloween. When summer comes, let the children have a leftover penny candy stand.

Cleanups: Your Child

❖   Take a baby to the sink using the "football hold" (tucked under your arm), and make a game of washing hands and face after meals.

❖   Put baby oil on your baby's face before feeding to facilitate cleanup later.

❖   Keep a step-stool handy for a child old enough to wash his or her own hands and face at the sink.

❖   Use your hand, dipped in water, to wash the face of a reluctant child. Most children don't seem to fight as much as if you use a cloth, and you'll do just as good a job.

❖ Let your child dip messy hands into a plastic bowl of water while still in the high chair. Then just wipe them dry.

❖ Squirt a little shaving cream on the child's cheeks and let him or her "shave" it off with a washcloth.

❖ Remove a "drink moustache" from your kid's face by rubbing toothpaste on it and rinsing it off. Kids usually like the pleasant taste and smell.

❖ Remove ink and magic marker stains from skin with baby wipes. Wipes are also good for removing stains like grape juice or cranberry juice and Coke from carpet and upholstery.

Cleanups: Equipment

❖ Put a plastic tablecloth or an old plastic shower curtain on the floor under the high chair, and wipe up spills easily. On a hard-surface floor, spread out a whole section of newspaper and pull off one page after each meal, wrapping the crumbs inside. Or get a nonfinicky dog!

❖ Mount a regular lightweight paper towel holder, or one with suction cups, on the back of the high chair to hold towels for quick cleanups.

❖ Buy a high chair with a detachable tray for easiest quick cleanups.

❖ Rub waxed paper over the runners of a clean high chair to make the tray slide back on more easily. Or apply a bit of petroleum jelly, nonstick vegetable oil, or WD-40.

❖ Clean the high chair tray easily with a few drops of shampoo that your toddler can play with after the meal, but while still in the high chair. After the child tires of "fingerpainting," clean up the tray and the child with the wipe of a sponge.

❖ Put a plastic or metal high chair under the shower, and let hot water spray over it for a few minutes. Caked-on food wipes off easily.

❖ Clean the high chair outdoors in the summer with the garden hose. Let it sit in the sun for a time to help disinfect it.

❖ Give your child an ice cream pail and a sponge and enlist "help" in the cleanup.

❖ Use a paper towel as a place mat for a child to make table cleanup easy.

❖   Use an old spray bottle filled with bleach (be sure to label it) or baking soda, and use it to get rid of stains on dishes, cups, and on the counter.

CLOTHING

As soon as possible, begin to give your child choices about clothes. Having a choice of two or three outfits can make all the difference with a finicky youngster and, for one who doesn't care, it provides practice in making decisions. This begins the process of establishing a self-image when dealing with a child-in-motion. Necklines in slip-over clothing must be large enough to slip over the child's head without a struggle. Preschoolers need plenty of pockets for collecting things. And remember, front fasteners will be easier for your child (and for you, when you are the dresser).

When You're the Dresser

❖   Buy overalls with fasteners in the crotch for easy diaper changing.

❖   Name clothes as you put them on and take them off.

❖   Play games such as "Peek-a-boo" and "Where Has Your Arm Gone?"

❖   To prevent straps from jumpers and overalls from sliding off shoulders, use a barrette to clip them closer together at the back. Or fasten overall straps in back with mitten clasps. Or criss-cross and pin them at the place they cross in the back.

❖   Run a bar of soap (the little ones from hotels are ideal) or a lead pencil over a sticking zipper.

When Your Child Is the Undresser

Don't be surprised if the toddler you just dressed removes all of his or her clothes within minutes. That's a skill to be mastered too. (One-piece garments will help discourage undressing, if you really don't have time for it.)

❖   For babies who like to take their diapers off, place elastic waist pants on or over the diapers.

❖   Or put diapers on backward so the tape's on the back side, making it harder for them to be removed.

❖ Consider changing to cloth diapers. They can be harder for the child to remove.

❖ To limit unzipping activity, secure the zipper lead to the cloth with a diaper pin.

❖ At night, put a child's one-piece sleeper on backwards. It will probably be necessary to cut off feet coverings, however.

Featuring Footed Items

❖ Stick T-shaped pieces of adhesive tape or nonslip bathtub appliqués on the bottoms of a baby's footed sleepers, socks, or slippers to give more traction and help a young walker gain confidence. One package of appliqués will last through several sleepers.

❖ If footed sleeper pj's are too warm for your child's feet, use a hole puncher to add ventilation holes to the soles.

❖ Make nonskid socks or sleeper feet for newly walking tots by painting on sock bottoms with a pen or tube that dries in a raised design.

❖ Slip wrist sweatbands around the ankles of sleeper pj's that are too long, to keep walking easier and safer.

Nighttime Diapering

❖ Double diaper a baby or toddler if you use cloth diapers, or put a sanitary pad (or part of one) inside a diaper.

❖ For a baby girl who sleeps on her stomach and leaks through disposables, use "boy" diapers that are extra absorbent in the front.

❖ Pull-on disposables and overnight sizes are available for older children who still wet the bed.

❖ Roll up a disposable diaper long ways (so the absorbent side faces out), and place it inside a cloth diaper like you would a sanitary pad.

Changing an Active Child

❖ Make changing time easier as your child becomes more active by having a special toy that comes out only at changing time. Give it to the baby the moment he or she is lying down.

❖ Change the baby in front of the TV so "Sesame Street" or the like can distract your child.

❖ Install an inexpensive shatterproof mirror over the changing table at the baby's eye level. The baby will watch the mirror and you'll have a hassle-free diaper change. Or put up mirror tiles where a child can see him- or herself.

❖ Or talk to the child very rapidly, so that he or she will have to pay close attention to your face, not your hands.

❖ Give the child a toothbrush to manipulate or a toy to play with, or stick some masking tape on his or her fingers—it will take a minute or two to get off.

❖ Dress a squirmy toddler face-down, if you can, for better control.

❖ Learn to change diapers on a standing child.

❖ Use diversions such as singing a favorite song or reciting a nursery rhyme to make changing easier.

❖ Use a hand puppet to do the "work" of changing and dressing. It can tell a story and amuse at the same time.

❖ Have your child hug you while you change the diaper.

❖ Bring the clothes to your child—not vice versa.

❖ When all else fails, tickle, tackle, and move very quickly!

For a Tot on the Crawl

❖ Put socks or booties on your crawling baby's hands to allow mobility while making it impossible to pick up and eat forbidden things.

❖ Use wrist sweatbands as knee protectors for crawling babies.

❖ Overalls and stretch suits stay in place better than separates that might get left behind as crawlers begin moving about.

Save Time ... Save Pajamas

Have your toddler dress at bedtime in tomorrow's clean clothes to sleep in, if you can bring yourself to break old habits. Today's fabrics don't wrinkle, and the kids are ready to go in the morning.

Dressing Themselves: Closings

You'll want to encourage your child's every effort at self-dressing, even though it will take a great deal more time at first and cause some frustration for both you and the child. Resist helping by keeping busy elsewhere, close enough to be of assistance if needed, but giving the child a chance to handle it alone.

❖ Make button-handling easier by sewing large buttons on your child's clothes where possible. Make it easier yet by sewing them on with elastic thread.

❖ Teach your child to button from the bottom up; chances of coming out even are better.

❖ Tie big wooden beads, buttons, or small toys to the strings of hoods to keep the strings from being pulled out.

❖ Attach notebook rings to zippers on boots and jackets to make them more manageable. On boots, the rings can be hooked together for storage.

❖ Teach your child to pull a zipper *away from* clothes and skin to keep it from catching.

❖ To help snaps work easier after washing and drying, spray each side of the snap with nonstick vegetable spray.

Dressing Themselves: Other Helps

❖ Buy pants and skirts with elasticized waistbands to make them easy to pull on and off, but be sure the elastic isn't so tight that it makes imprints on the skin or rides up.

❖ Mark the belt hole a child should use with a piece of masking or adhesive tape.

❖ Try to get clothing with monograms, appliqués, or other special trim on the front to help a child tell the front from the back. On homemade garments, mark an X on the back with colored thread.

❖ Teach your child to look for the label in the back of underpants. If there's no label, indicate the front by sewing on a "belly button" or drawing one with a marking pen.

XYZ!

You have a boy who's often caught with his zipper down? Say "XYZ" to him—"Examine your zipper." Add "PDQ"—"Pretty darn quick!"

Outerwear

❖ Put a small treat such as a raisin or piece of dry cereal into your child's hand so he or she will make a fist to push through a sleeve.

❖ Sew loops of elastic thread inside the cuffs of sweaters and have your child lap them over the thumbs to hold sleeves down while putting on a coat or jacket.

❖ Attach mittens to a long string that goes through both coat sleeves if your toddler can undo mitten clips.

❖ Use knee-high socks as mittens—they can't be pulled off.

❖ Clip mittens together with clothespins to keep track of them when not in use.

❖ Put a pair of surgical gloves or dishwashing gloves over warm dry gloves. If gloves stay dry, hands stay warm.

❖ Encourage your child to always slip one mitten or glove inside the other one when taking them off. When you find one, the other will be there.

❖ Clothespin wet mittens onto a hanger and hang over a register to dry.

❖ Hang snowsuits to dry, or tumble-dry in a dryer. To prevent clumping of "fill," throw a tennis ball or a sneaker into the dryer.

❖ To insulate or "fill-in" boots a bit too big, cut a piece of carpet or even a piece of styrofoam from a food tray to fit the inside sole.

❖ Use your portable hair dryer to dry winter boots quickly.

❖ Help your child put on a jacket or coat: spread the garment on the floor, openings up, and have the child stand above it at the neck end, bend over, slip arms into sleeves, and flip it over the head. Or have the child lie on his or her back on the garment, put arms in armholes and stand up.

Putting Shoes On

❖ Put shoes on a squirmy toddler while the child is in the high chair. Or lightly tickle the bottom of the child's foot—toes will uncurl and shoes will go on smoothly.

❖ Use mitten clips to attach baby's shoes to hem of pants so if shoes are kicked off, they are not lost.

❖ Wet shoelaces before tying them, and as they dry they'll tighten up and stay tied. Better yet, look for shoes with Velcro fasteners.

❖ Prevent the tongues of shoes from sliding out of place by cutting two small parallel slits in each tongue, a half-inch from the outside tip. Pull the laces through the slots and tie as usual.

❖ Put plastic bags over shoes before putting on boots, for ease of entry. The bags will help keep shoes dry, too. They can be stapled into the boots if you like.

❖ Cover shoes with large woolen socks to keep your child's feet extra warm and dry inside boots. Buy boots large enough to accommodate the extra layer.

Helping with Shoes

Shoes are not obligatory for new walkers. Going barefoot gives little feet good exercise. For a child a little older, new shoes are often a great source of pleasure. They can also be a source of frustration. To help your child distinguish between the right and left shoes, mark the inside edges of both shoes with tape or a colored marker; when marks face each other, the shoes are on the right feet. Or explain that if toes point in, shoes "like each other" and are happy; when they point away from each other, they're sad. You can also mark inside heel soles with an L and R or a design to match up shoes in their proper postion. And one last variation: draw a design on front of sneakers, one-half on each shoe, so the puzzle matches up.

❖ Coat the ends of shoelaces with clear nail polish or wrap them with masking tape when the plastic tips wear off.

❖ Tie knots in shoestrings after the first two holes are laced. Or tie knots in the end of the laces. The child can remove the shoes easily but won't pull the laces out.

❖ Avoid lacing and tying problems by substituting quarter-inch elastic for laces. Sew ends together at the top. The elastic stretches so that the shoe can be slipped on and off without untying.

❖ Keep shoelaces even at the ends by tying knots at their centers.

❖ Place two pieces of masking tape or nonslip bathtub appliqués on the soles of newly bought slippery shoes. Or apply a small amount of glue with a glue gun in a zigzag pattern to prevent slipping. Some shoe bottoms can be given extra traction by just going over them with a piece of sandpaper or by scoring the bottoms with the tip of a scissors.

❖ Trace your child's footprint on sturdy cardboard. Carry it as a guide when you're shopping without your child and you see a great shoe bargain. You should be able to slip the footprint into the shoe.

Keeping Clothes Organized

❖ Hang coordinated sets of clothes in the closet, or put complete outfits together in bureau drawers so that your child can select matching outfits.

❖ Organize socks for more than one child by assigning a special pattern or color to each child, or by buying a different brand for each.

❖ Buy all socks in the same brand and color for an only child to save the trouble of matching them.

❖ Pin pairs of tiny socks together with diaper pins for laundry and storage, and pin them to the clothesline.

❖ Identify children's clothes with an indelible pen, a liquid embroidery pen, an inexpensive rubber stamp, or fabric paint pens.

❖ Write names on dark colored boots and rubbers with a cotton swab dipped in bleach or with red nail polish. If you prefer to mark inside the boots, use a marking pen.

❖ Use small hanging pocket bags, shelves, or drawers for storing shoes.

❖ Sort clean laundry into colored baskets. Each family member is assigned a certain color and will know which pile of laundry is his or hers to fold and put away.

Hand-Me-Downs

❖ Mark borrowed babies' or children's clothes that are to be returned so you'll remember the lender. And label things you lend and want returned.

❖ Sort hand-me-downs according to season and size, and label the boxes in which they're stored. Use disposable diaper boxes or bags that designate weight or size to store appropriate baby clothes and small items. Really precious baby things (the ones you want to save forever) will be better preserved in self-closing plastic bags.

❖ Make boys' hand-me-downs feminine for girls by embroidering initials on pockets and designs around collars or cuffs and/or sewing on appliqués.

❖ Change hand-me-downs so they're special for your child.

❖ Mark clothes with a single X or dot for the oldest child, two for the next, and so on. When clothes are handed down, it's easy to add another mark.

❖ Mark sizes on the inside waistbands of pants if labels have come off or become unreadable.

❖ Use the family last name only for marking outer clothes that you're sure will be handed down from one child to another.

❖ Avoid resentment over hand-me-downs by calling them "hand-me-overs," or "kindergarten dresses" or "first grade pants" instead of "Susie's dresses" or "Jimmy's pants." Approach it as a positive sign of how much the child has grown.

Wise Shopping for Clothing

Some of the best-dressed children have the least amount of money spent on their clothes. Garage sales, thrift shops, discount stores, and manufacturers' outlet stores account for some savings (and thrift shops will take *your* children's used clothing for sale on consignment). Hand-me-downs from relatives and friends also help. Clever shoppers try to keep a little cash on hand for an unexpected opportunity. Carrying a small notebook with measurements and sizes of all family members helps, too. For small children height and weight measurements are often more important than sizes. Remember to update your notebook often.

❖   Don't buy plastic pants with snaps; they rip off too easily.

❖   Buy "neutral" jeans, shirts, and outer clothing so that they can be passed on to children of different sexes.

❖   Get unisex clothing in boys' departments; it's usually more rugged and often costs less than items in girls' departments.

❖   Buy best quality in everyday wear such as underwear and in items that will be passed on to several children.

❖   Check for fit in socks if you aren't sure of size: have the child make a fist and wrap the sock around the fist over the knuckles. If the heel and toe meet, the sock will fit.

❖   Or buy tube socks. They wear evenly, are easy to put on, and "grow" with kids.

❖   Buy shoes with laces or Velcro closings for small children. Little slip-ons are cute and easy to put on, but they often don't *stay* on.

❖   Try two-piece grow-a-size pajamas. If you always stick with the same color and brand, you can use good parts of worn-out ones for patches.

❖   Or consider using bright T-shirts with iron-on transfers or embroidery for nightshirts.

❖   Buy smock-type dresses for girls; when they're too short they become tops to be worn over pants.

❖ Remember when you buy snowsuits that while one piece gar ments are easier to put on, two-piece suits can be worn longer.

Home-Sewn

"Get a good sewing machine and learn to use it, and learn to knit and crochet," is the advice of many parents who want their kids to be dressed well and economically. Work ahead of the seasons, they advise; think about hats and mittens and jackets in the summer, shorts and sundresses in winter. Don't put hems in until it's time for kids to wear the garments.

You can allow for growth by choosing styles with raglan or dolman sleeves and, in one-piece garments, with undefined waistlines. If you make double-breasted coats and jackets, you can realign buttons as the child grows.

❖ To accurately measure children for clothing, lay them on their backs on the material and measure or pin the length of arms and legs.

❖ Wash (*always*) all fabric before cutting to allow for shrinkage and for bleeding of colors. Use the water temperature and dry- ing method you'll use for the finished garment.

❖ Sew on shank buttons and metal overall buttons with dental floss to keep them from being torn off.

❖ Apply clear nail polish over the tops of small buttons to help keep them from coming off and perhaps finding their way into a small child's mouth.

❖ Avoid sewing on buttons when you know you'll be moving them as a child grows. Sew thread through button eyes as if you're sewing the button onto cloth. Attach the buttons to the garment with safety pins run through the thread on the back . . . and repin as necessary.

❖ Sew an extra button under the hem of a front-buttoning gar- ment so that you'll have a matching one when the garment is lengthened.

❖ Sew an extra button or two to a piece of fabric from a garment and store it in your button box for easy replacement.

❖ Use cellophane tape or masking tape when you're measuring

and marking hems; it won't pinch or stab your child as pins will.

❖ Save handwork by using iron-on bonding materials for hems in lightweight fabrics.

❖ Put a long zipper from top to crotch in overalls for a boy who's toilet trained. A standard fly is usually hard to manipulate.

❖ Use empty vitamin bottles or other small containers with childproof caps to store pins and other little sewing notions. Contents are easily visible, yet safe from children.

Uses for Wonderful Velcro

❖ In small circles, in place of buttons, down the fronts of shirts and blouses and for waistband closures.

❖ Instead of buttons, to attach overall straps to overall bibs.

❖ Attached to mittens, to stick them together for storage.

❖ On overall straps in the back, to keep them from slipping down a child's arms.

❖ On washcloths, to make easy-to-change diapers for your child's baby doll.

❖ To make a "custom" T-shirt, attaching tiny stuffed animals or other little toys that your child can take on and off.

Making Clothes Last Longer

❖ Buy two-piece blanket sleepers for longer wear, and when they're too short, extend their lives by cutting the feet off.

❖ Open the bottom seam of an outgrown one-piece blanket sleeper, and use it for a beach coverup.

❖ Try tie-dying T-shirts that are badly stained.

❖ Put extra buttons on overall straps at longer lengths than a child needs. As he or she grows, the old ones can simply be snipped off. And sew double rows of snaps or buttons on two-piece sleepwear for the same reason.

❖ Lengthen girls' slacks by sewing on strips of grosgrain ribbon or decorative braid. Add similar trim or ruffles to the legs of pajama pants, or cut off sleeves and legs to make summer pajamas.

❖ Lengthen suspender straps by sewing on extra fabric.

❖ Add another tier to tiered skirts or jumpers, using matching or contrasting fabric.

❖ Cut the too-short sleeves out of an expensive quilted or padded jacket and let your child wear it as a vest over a heavy sweater.

❖ Extend the wear of jackets and snowsuits by sewing knitted cuffs (from the notions departments in fabric stores) to the ends of the sleeves.

Patching and Covering Up

❖ Patch the knees and feet of blanket sleepers with pieces of an old flannel-backed tablecloth.

❖ Cover old hemline marks on skirts or pants with zigzag stitching or sewn-on rickrack or ribbon bands.

❖ Run a dark blue crayon or indelible pencil over the white line on let-down jeans.

❖ Slip a rolled-up magazine into pants legs to avoid running through both thicknesses of material when pinning on patches.

❖ Or hold patches in place for stitching by gluing them on first. After sewing, wash the glue out.

❖ Cover a hole, mend, or stain that shows by sewing on an appliqué.

Knit Knacks

❖ Crochet mittens onto the sleeves of a sweater, and they'll never get lost or separated.

❖ Use a pattern one size larger than your child needs when you knit or crochet a garment. If it takes a long time to finish, there's a better chance it will still fit.

Preventive Maintenance

❖ Spray knees, cuffs, and collars of garments with fabric protector (and the fronts of "best clothes" for a drooler or messy eater). Spills will bead up, and dirt can be wiped off with a damp cloth.

❖ Sew squares of quilted material on the knees of pants for crawling babies; they protect both pants and knees. Use pant iron patches *inside* knees—even on tough pants.

❖ Put iron-on patches on the cotton soles of sleepers to keep them from wearing out.

❖ Reinforce the knees on new jeans (on the inside) with iron-on patches or with the extra fabric you trim from too-long legs.

Getting Clothes Clean

Today almost everything but the child goes into the washing machine. Bleach of one kind or another does wonders with really dirty clothes. Some parents change brands of laundry detergent occasionally, feeling that the new brand washes out the residue of the old, and clothes will be cleaner. If you take your laundry to a laundromat, carry your detergent in old baby food jars or self-closing plastic bags to lighten the load you must drag along. And remember there's no law that says kids' play clothes must be spotless!

❖ Get grimy socks white by soaking them in a solution of washing soda and water before laundering. Yes, bleach works, too. Or boil them in water with a sliced lemon.

❖ Soak egg-stained clothing in cold water for an hour before laundering. Hot water will set the stain.

❖ Soak vomit-stained clothes in cold water, and sponge stains with a solution of a quart of ammonia and a half teaspoon of liquid detergent.

❖ Use bottled rug shampoo with a brush (and lots of suds) for winter coats that need dry cleaning. It works on both wool and corduroy.

❖ Pour boiling water through grape juice stained areas of clothing.

❖ Place a piece of wax paper over gum on clothing or fabric. Run a warm iron over area. The gum will quickly "melt" onto the waxed paper. Or use masking tape to lift it off.

Kid-Created Stains

Something our moms failed to tell us about—probably because we didn't care then—were the joys (?) and frustrations of continual laundry. Suddenly we need to become experts in stain removal as well as keeping mounds of clothes in motion as they go from clean to dirty to clean.

Over the years, other people have recommended the following items for stain removal. I will not vouch for each of them. So often their effectiveness depends on the nature and age of the stain and on the nature of what has been stained. Consider the following list as options you may wish to try. No doubt one or more will work for you.

Ballpoint pen/ink: Hairspray
Toothpaste and toothbrush
Vinegar on painted surfaces

Blood stains: Hydrogen peroxide
A paste of meat tenderizer
Shampoo rubbed in, then cold water wash
WHINK rust remover

Grass stains: Alcohol
Shampoo
Simple Green
Tilex bathroom cleaner
Treat with a prewash soak overnight, then wash using bleach
Toothpaste and toothbrush
White wall tire cleaner

Grease: Baby/talc powder, then brush off
Baking soda
Club soda
Crisco
Go-Jo
Oven cleaner

Spills/stains: Baby wipes
                          Baking soda
                          Bleach on a cotton swab
                          Club soda
                          Liquid dishwasher detergent
                          Murphy's Oil Soap
                          Oven cleaner
                          Rubbing alcohol
                          Shaving cream
                          Toilet bowl cleaner
                          Toothpaste and toothbrush
                          Upholstery cleaner
                          Window spray

Caring for Shoes

❖ Clean white baby shoes by rubbing them with a raw potato,
   liquid nonabrasive cleaner, or alcohol before polishing. Or
   apply toothpaste with an old toothbrush, scrub gently, and
   wipe off. Let shoes dry before polishing.

❖ Spray newly polished white baby shoes with hair spray to prevent polish from coming off.

❖ Use baby wipes to remove black marks from white shoes.

❖ Remove gum from the bottom of shoes by putting them in the
   freezer. Scrape the gum off when it's frozen.

❖ Make white canvas shoes white again by washing them and
   polishing them with white shoe polish. Let them air dry.

❖ To keep the soles of shoes from being stained with polish, paint
   the edges with clear nail polish.

❖ Use hair spray on stains on tennis shoes. Spray, leave for a
   few seconds and wipe with a soft cloth. Or try toothpaste and
   a toothbrush or a soap-filled scouring pad. Use bleach or
   lemon juice in the rinse water if the shoes are white. Even
   foam bathroom tile and basin cleaner can be effective on
   leather sneakers.

❖ Spray new sneakers with Scotch-guard fabric protector to keep dirt from becoming embedded. Grass stains and mud will come out easier. Spray after every wash.

❖ Clean the bottom of children's tennis shoes by using an old toothbrush or potato scrubber. Rinse under warm running water.

❖ Ensure dry tennis shoes by morning by placing them on their sides in front of the refrigerator. The fan should produce constant warm air to dry them.

SLEEPING

Getting children to sleep comfortably and fearlessly through the night is a problem most parents have at one time or another. Just wait though— teenagers usually sleep very well, and often late into the morning when you'd like them to be up and about.

Determining Bedtime

❖ Keep bedtime at the *same* time every night to help establish regular sleep habits.

❖ Relieve yourself of the onus of setting bedtime by letting the hands of the clock do the job, or set a timer to mark bedtime and let it go off early enough to give a little warning. Leftover time might be added to the bedtime ritual as a reward for hurrying.

❖ Have a "Goodnight Parade" if you have two or more children. The whole family marches through the house, stopping in the kitchen for water, in the bathroom for toothbrushing and toileting, in the living room to lock the front door for the night. The "Caboose" (youngest) is dropped off first.

❖ Or have your child put all toys to bed, one by one, and when they're all down, he or she is the *last one* to go to bed.

Helping Children Get to Sleep

❖ Use the five- or ten-minute check for the child afraid to be left alone at night. When the child goes to bed, agree to come back every five to ten minutes until he or she is asleep. Just knowing you'll be back helps a child relax. Or work or clean up in the next room so your child hears you nearby.

❖ Feed your older child a protein snack, if you offer a snack at all, before bedtime. (P.S. Milk is protein.)

❖ Have quiet time before bedtime. Rough-and-tumble play excites a child, making it hard to settle down into sleep.

❖ Take a long walk with your child in the evening, followed by a nice warm bath and some soothing music.

❖ Continue the sleep routine you started when your child was an infant. Or create a new routine. But do have a routine.

❖ Put a few favorite dolls or stuffed animals in bed with your child and tell him or her the toys are ready to settle down. The child may cooperate by settling down him- or herself.

❖ Let even a little child "read" him- or herself to sleep lying down—with a pleasant, nonscary book and maybe an accompanying audio tape.

❖ Don't use a crib or bed as a place for punishment.

❖ Put soft stereo headphones on an older child, and let restful music induce sleep. Be sure cords are atop head, not around the neck. Or set a clock radio that will turn off on its own.

❖ Give your child a relaxing mini massage.

❖ Add interest to a child's back rub by "planting a garden," using different strokes for spading, raking, preparing the rows, and planting the seeds of fruits and vegetables the child selects.

❖ Teach your child to relax every muscle, starting with the toes and moving up to the head. Eyes should be kept closed.

❖ Put a dab of cologne on the back of your child's hand and tell him or her to sniff until the scent is gone. Deep breathing and concentration usually bring sleep quickly.

❖ Let your child pick from a Dream Jar (perhaps an empty can you've decorated) a slip of paper on which you've written an idea for a pleasant dream. The child can go to sleep with the paper beneath the pillow.

Bedtime Storytelling

❖ Relate a true event about the child or family (the night they were born, or you were born, what you did as a child). Encourage good behavior by using a favorite doll as a story hero. Tell a fill-in-the-blank story ("You and I were just ready to cross the street . . . and then what happened?"). Remember to keep the stories short, as children's attention spans are limited, and the central character should be familiar.

❖ Tell your child stories in which he or she is the hero such as Lady Dana and Sir Douglas. Use common childhood stories, your imagination, or change characters names in books to those of your child. Or investigate the specially printed, personalized books that use the names of the child, siblings, friends, and pets.

❖ When reading storybooks to your children, use correction fluid over the character's names and fill in the names of your own children.

Night Wakers

Some parents let a wakeful child cry after checking to make sure there's nothing really wrong, and they say the crying shortens in duration over a few nights and soon stops altogether. Check your clock rather than your gut feeling. It always feels like children are crying longer than they actually are. If you can't bear to do that, keep in mind that often simply rubbing a child's back or reassuring him or her from the door every five minutes will do the trick. Avoid picking up or rocking your child or giving an unnecessary bottle. Children have to learn to calm themselves for sleep. If you choose to do it for them, they will continue to let you.

❖ Give your child a bottle if you wish, but if he or she has teeth, make it plain water only. Milk or any sweetened drink may lead to severe tooth decay.

❖ Keep several pacifiers in the crib, but *never* tie one on a string around a baby's neck or crib bar. It might get tangled and cause strangulation.

❖ Take the child back to bed with you. One "family bed" variation is a king-size bed with a one-side-removed crib pushed up against it. Another is a guard rail on one side of the bed; the parents needn't be separated with a child between them, yet there's no worry about the child falling out of bed. For some, family sleeping equals comfort. Those who like the idea (not everyone does!) say it fulfills a basic human need for warmth, closeness, and security.

❖ Use an incentive chart for a child if you don't want company in your bed. Draw stars on a calendar with marking pens (let the child choose the color) for each night he or she doesn't come to your bed. Ten stars might earn a small present.

❖ Put a small mattress, futon, or a big pillow and a blanket on the floor near your bed for the nighttime waker who needs to fall back asleep near you.

❖ Satisfy a thirsty toddler by taping a car drink holder to the crib railing to hold a nonspill cup with juice or water in it. Your child won't have to wake you for a drink.

❖ Use a night light in the room if the child wants one, or let the child have a flashlight. Or try a lighted fish tank, which offers not only light but movement and the soft sounds of bubbling as well. A bed light with a dimmer switch can allow an older child to read a little and then get back to sleep without getting out of bed.

Delaying the Early Riser

❖ Put a few cloth books or soft toys in a small child's crib for morning play. But do it after the child is asleep.

❖ Attach an unbreakable mirror to the inside of the crib so a baby or toddler can amuse him- or herself for a few extra minutes in the morning.

❖ Leave a "surprise bag" (*never* a plastic one) by the bed of an older child or fasten a bicycle basket or plastic pail to the side of the crib also after the child is asleep. Put in any selection of small items for quiet play—books, games, or things to create with.

❖ Add a bite to eat for a child who will be hungry and who can handle eating without supervision. One good snack that consumes a great deal of time is a Cheerios snake: Tear two to three inches of waxed paper from a roll, fold lengthwise, then place a few Cheerios in the fold at one end, twist paper to hold in Cheerios, place a few more pieces in next section of waxed paper, twist paper to hold in more pieces, and continue until you have a "snake" or "necklace" full of Cheerios. Your child must untwist each section to get at the next batch of Cheerios. (Some parents won't put food out, feeling that it may attract undesirable animals or insects.)

❖ Set an alarm clock or clock radio for one who *always* wakes early. When it goes off, he or she may get up. Or set up two clocks for a preschooler, one running, the other unwound and set at getting-up time. When the hands of the second match those of the first, the child may get up.

❖ Set your TV/VCR with a favorite video that your child can turn on, even if this is done in your bedroom. (Preset the volume down if you can.)

❖ Or time a small TV or radio to go on in your child's room at whatever all-too-early hour he or she usually arises.

❖ Give up! Accept your child's body rhythms. Perhaps there's a 24-hour grocery near you, and you can do something constructive during these extra wakeful hours.

Naps

❖ Try white noise in a little one's room if older non-nappers' playing keeps him or her from sleeping. Set up a small fan on a high dresser, directing the flow of air away from the child, and let it hum away.

❖ Make a naptime nook for a toddler in a large cardboard box decorated with bright drawings or decals inside and padded comfortably.

❖ Let your child nap in a sleeping bag on your bed, the family room couch, or the floor of his or her own room, just for variety.

❖ Call naptime by another name such as "rest time" or "quiet time" for a child who resists sleeping. Sometimes the child will actually fall asleep, but even if he or she doesn't, the time alone will be relaxing.

❖ Set a clock radio alarm to play music for a resting child, or put on a single soft audio tape. The end of the music marks the end of rest time. Children usually drop off long before the music does.

❖ Read a book or two to your child as part of a naptime routine.

❖ Have a toy that can be played with only at naptime.

❖ Wake a too-long napping child to the sound of favorite music.

Going Visiting?

The friend you're visiting doesn't have a crib—and your *nonmobile* infant needs a nap? Settle the baby down in the bathtub with a big cushion or a few soft towels for a mattress! Be sure to remove soap and other bathing equipment!

CHAPTER 3

Hygiene and Health

Parents of young children usually spend a good deal of time in the bathroom . . . but not by themselves! Trying to keep active kids clean, introducing them to the art of cleaning themselves, and getting them to use the toilet are time-consuming operations. Here are some ideas to make that time pay off.

SOAP AND WATER

When there are two or more little bodies to be bathed (or even just one), many parents find the assembly line method fast and easy. One parent washes and shampoos, the other dries and assists with pajamas.

Bathing and Shampooing

❖ Use a clean plastic syrup bottle or dishwashing detergent bottle as a baby shampoo dispenser. The pull-up top lets you squirt just the right amount and close it with one hand. Or keep baby shampoo in a hand-pump soap container (that you label with a permanent marker). It allows you always to keep one hand on a slippery baby.

❖ Take your child into the shower with you to help accustom a child to water on the head and face.

❖ Strap a baby into an infant seat with a towel replacing the pad if you use a big tub for a baby who can't sit alone.

❖ Place the baby bathtub in the regular tub when your baby is not big enough to sit up in a bathtub. It helps keep an active infant in place and keep your floor dry.

❖ Let a child who can sit upright play in a small, open mesh plastic laundry basket in the big tub as a transition from the baby bathtub. The basket can serve as a place to store the bath toys when the bath is finished. An older child might prefer sitting on a plastic booster seat in the middle of the tub.

❖ Or try using a plastic inflatable pool in the shower stall, also as a transition.

Removing Grass Stains

To get rid of summer grass stains on little feet, rub each foot with half a lemon for about a minute or so.

Making It Fun

❖ For face cleaning, a puppet washcloth on your hand makes cleanup less traumatic.

❖ Offer a "smelly" bath using flavor extracts. Peppermint extract and red food coloring are fun.

❖ Help teach a little girl to get herself clean in the bath by pretending she is a big girl getting ready to go to a party. Soap on face is cream, powder, blush, and eye makeup; on legs are silk stockings; on arms are white satin gloves.

❖ Create a fun washcloth from an unmatched sock for you or your child to use at bathtime. It's washable, while foaming bath mitts are not.

❖ Add a face to the above sock with permanent markers.

Play in the Bath

There are many bathroom activities to keep you occupied while your child is happily at play in the tub. Clean the room (toilets, cabinets, or mirrors); work on yourself (polish nails, shave legs, sharpen eye liners); work on your "to-do" list (clip coupons, read mail, plan your grocery list);

or read the newspaper.

* Store bath toys in a large, plastic planter. They are sturdy, have drain holes, come in many colors, and are inexpensive.

* Keep bath toys in a nylon net bag, and hang it from a faucet or shower head to drip dry.

* Toss small rubber bathtub toys in the washing machine next time you launder your shower curtain. A bit of bleach will kill mildew and germs. Run on gentle cycle.

* Or clean grungy bathtub toys by soaking them overnight in a bucket of water with a cup of bleach and a dash of detergent.

* Make inexpensive bath toys by cutting colored sponges into interesting shapes.

* Let bathtime be "science time": provide a variety of things that sink and float; plastic glasses tall and thin, short and fat; large and small cups for measuring and pouring.

* Let it be snack time. One cookie can be a good distraction.

* If your toddler hates to leave the tub, pull the plug. When there's no more water for play, he or she will probably leave willingly. Or set a timer to go off when playtime is over.

* Or make simple rules: "You're through when you stand up," or "You're through when your skin is wrinkled and you look like a raisin."

BATHTUB SAFETY!
Never leave a small child unattended in a bathtub—
even if an older sibling is present!

Fear of the Bath Water

* Bathe with your small child to provide extra security . . . and besides, it's fun!

❖ Run the bath water before bringing a frightened child into the bathoom if you don't have another child who might climb in while your back is turned.

❖ Ask questions to find out what is scaring your child—the volume? The drain? A slippery tub?

❖ Lure those who are reluctant to get into the bath by putting creamy hand lotion in some little cups and mixing a few drips of food coloring in each. Have the children use the concoction to "paint" their face and body, then have them hop into the tub.

❖ Ask your child to help you put in a nonskid mat, lots of toys, and bubble bath for diversions. Some parents prefer to use a little liquid dishwashing detergent for bubbles. (Commercial bubble bath has been known to contribute to vaginal infection in little girls if used too often.)

❖ Use only a few inches of water in the tub, increasing the amount as your child gets more comfortable with the water.

❖ Swimming and swimming classes often help kids overcome bathtub fears.

Scared of Shampooing

Most first-time parents are surprised when a fear of shampooing develops, yet it's common. Shampoo as seldom as possible during this period. Once or twice a week is probably often enough, unless your child has special problems. You can make a game out of hair washing by joining your child in the bathtub and pouring water over your own head first, or let your child wash a doll's hair while you wash his or hers. Don't force the issue or try to *prove* it doesn't hurt. Instead, brush hair frequently (you can cover the hairbrush with an old nylon stocking to help absorb oils), and occasionally wash hair with a damp washcloth. When you must shampoo, use a no-sting baby shampoo, and do the job quickly and matter-of-factly, praising your child for bravery. As difficult as this period is for you both, remember that it will pass.

Making Shampooing Easier

❖ Shampoo your child first, and then allow for playtime so the bath will end on a happy note.

❖ Try letting someone else be the shampooer (father, aunt, etc.).

❖ Make soap sculptures in the hair with shampoo, and keep a hand mirror handy so that the child can admire them and watch the whole process.

❖ Try reintroducing a no-longer-used infant seat; the tilt allows the child's head to be tipped back comfortably for shampooing.

❖ Tell your child the story of a speck of dirt that gets tired, settles for a nap on the child's head, and is joined by lots more specks, only to get washed out by Mom or Dad. The ritual of the story should last as long as the shampoo does.

❖ Or sing loud songs together throughout the whole shampoo process.

❖ Wrap the child in a big beach towel and lay him or her on the kitchen counter, face up, with head over the sink. Use a sink spray, if one's available. The towel holds the child steady, it is easier for you to control the soap and water, and your closeness gives security.

❖ Put only a small amount of water in the tub so the child can lie down flat for shampooing.

❖ Fill a big plastic jug with water and let it sink to the bottom of the tub. The child can use it for a headrest.

❖ Or use your arm to support the child's head while leaning back.

❖ Have the child lean back under the faucet for a quick, easy rinse. Or make it fun by using his or her own little watering can for the rinse.

❖ Give your hands and sponge names and have them argue over who's going to wash the child's hair.

❖ Let the child control the hand-held shower massager.

Keeping Shampoo Out of Little Eyes

❖ Place colorful stickers on the ceiling over your tub to get your child's attention so you can rinse shampoo suds off. Change stickers periodically if interest seems to wane.

❖ Use a sponge instead of a cup to control water when you rinse. (And try a sponge for applying shampoo. Soap won't be so likely to run into eyes.)

❖ Give your child a small folded towel or washcloth to hold over his or her face. Or use a plastic visor. Create a disposable shampooing visor by cutting out the inside circle of a paper plate so the rim will deflect soap and water.

❖ Use swim goggles to prevent soap and water from getting into eyes. Make a game of it by telling your child he or she looks like a frog. Have your child repeat, "Ribbit!"

To Remove Gum from Hair

Use peanut butter. Work it into hair, comb out gum and peanut butter. Shampoo. Cold cream also works, as do olive oil and witch hazel. (And try baby oil to remove gum from skin, or press a second wad of gum over the first and lift both off together.)

For Girls' Hair Only

❖ Use transparent tape to attach a bow to a hairless baby girl's head (works on fine hair, too).

❖ Iron hair ribbons by sweeping them through a hot curling iron.

❖ Use yarn, long shoelaces, and pipe cleaners as well as ribbon to decorate hair.

❖ Clip barrettes on a long ribbon and hang in the bathroom or wherever you fix your child's hair.

❖ Slip hair ribbons through a coated rubber band. Use the rubber band on your child's hair, and the ribbons won't fall off and get lost.

❖ Wrap unused elastic bands around the handle of a hairbrush.

❖ Spray ribbons with hair spray to keep them stiff.

❖ Use spray-on conditioner after shampooing for long, tangled hair.

❖ Rub a fabric softener sheet over static-ridden flyaway hair.

❖ Count the number of brush strokes with your child as you brush long hair to distract her.

CLEAN AND NEAT

As children grow, they often begin to take pleasure in looking nice and smelling good. If they start out with serviceable habits, they'll be apt to stick with them. Remember that with babies and toddlers, the finer points of grooming are your responsibility, and you don't want to encourage self-help with such tools as scissors and cotton swabs.

Encouraging Good Habits

❖ Keep a sturdy step stool next to the sink to encourage self-help.

❖ Hang a small medicine cabinet on the bathroom wall at child's eye level to hold grooming necessities. If the small cabinet is mirrored, so much the better.

❖ Or buy mirror tiles you can stick on the wall at child height so your child won't have to climb. If possible, position the tiles where you can add additional ones above them as the child grows.

❖ Give your child an inexpensive plastic carrying case with his or her name on it to use as a personal hygiene kit. Equip it with a travel-size tube of toothpaste, a toothbrush, a small bar of soap, and other necessities.

❖ Half fill your bathroom sink each morning with clean water and let your kid just dip his or her hands in, use soap, and towel dry, to simplify the washing process. Change water as needed.

❖ Ask your child, when washing with soap and water, "Are all those little germies gone?" It helps them conceptualize "stuff" on their hands that must be washed off.

❖ Give a bath mitt to a child who hates to wash up. Make one out of an old sock tied up with soap inside or small leftover pieces, or sew two washcloths together and put soap chips inside.

❖   A liquid soap dispenser is probably *not* a good idea until children are about five and will not use it as a plaything.

Using Hand Towels

The best way to get really dirty hands clean is to have a child wash something in the sink: a toy, a doll, some plastic cups. Remember that you really like a wet, dirty towel better than a neatly hung, unused one in the bathroom.

❖   Consider assigning each member of the family towels of different colors.

❖   Or buy washcloths and hand towels printed with pictures of favorite storybook characters for the kids.

❖   Place press-on hooks at your child's level so that towels can be hung up more easily.

❖   Or attach a hand towel to a towel bar with a shower curtain ring. It will hang securely for hand drying.

Cutting Nails

❖   Cut an infant's nails at nursing time, with his or her head propped on a pillow so that you have both hands free, or cut nails while the infant or child is asleep.

❖   Use round-ended scissors, for safety's sake. Or try a nail clipper; some say it's easier to use than scissors. (Try keeping one on your key ring for quick clips when the baby sleeps while you're away from home.)

❖   Put baby powder in your palm and scrape your child's nails over it. Enough will stick under the nails to show you how far to cut without hurting the baby.

❖   Put a squirmy toddler in the high chair and give him or her something to eat. Or cut nails right after a meal, when the child is sleepy and content, or let your child watch television as a distraction while you cut his or her nails.

❖   Try filing a child's nails instead.

❖   Clean under little nails with a flat wooden toothpick.

Cutting Hair

Keep in mind that time is of the essence when cutting hair. Use sharp shears. The job will go faster. What can't be done in five minutes probably won't get done. Keep your child occupied by talking and letting him or her watch what is going on in a mirror. Try to insist that haircutting is a job for adults *only*. If your preschooler abides by this rule, you'll be lucky!

❖ Wait until your little one is so tired he or she will fall asleep in the high chair. Then, work your magic by cutting the baby's hair while he or she sleeps. Results may not be high style, but the bulk of it will be off without a scene.

❖ Call a haircut a "trim." *Cuts* hurt! Talk about "fixing" or "making hair pretty."

❖ Set a child in a high chair or on a high stool outdoors in the summer. Spread newspaper to catch falling hair, even outdoors, because hair doesn't disintegrate as yard clippings do.

❖ Wrap a child in a large beach towel or small sheet when cutting hair to keep falling hair from slipping down the shirt and becoming itchy.

❖ Or let the child wear a Halloween mask, which will keep hair from eyes. Be sure to have a mirror handy so the child can admire the effect.

❖ Try cutting hair with electric hair clippers (they tickle!). If Mom cuts Dad's hair with them too, it helps kids to see that *he* isn't scared. And if a child is good, end the haircut on a high note with a few drops of cologne.

❖ Provide your child with a clean squirt water bottle (like the stylist uses) that can be used to spray on his or her own hair, or even into the mouth or face. Your child's that is, not yours.

❖ Trimming bangs? Use a visor cap and trim the hair over it so the hair falls away from the face. Remember that hair bounces up when dry, so allow an extra quarter to a half inch.

❖ Or place a piece of cardboard or paper between the child's hair and forehead to keep hair snips and the cold scissors away from the face.

❖ Trying to cut bangs straight? Dampen hair with a spritzer (conditioner can be helpful), imagine a line drawn from outer eyebrow to outer eyebrow, and use your comb to hold the hair in place while you trim across. Hold your child's head steady by having your hand hold the chin.

❖ Put a piece of transparent tape (or special hair tape, which pulls off easily) across bangs and cut evenly above it.

❖ Keep children quiet while fixing their hair by letting them play with something that is usually forbidden (costume jewelry, a deck of cards, etc.).

❖ Play beauty parlor. For girls, a reward for sitting still can be having one's nails polished. (Even boys like clear polish.)

❖ Strap your toddler into a car seat on the kitchen table and turn the TV on to a favorite show or special video. Make a special event out of it, and it will distract your child while you cut his or her hair.

❖ Cut hair in the bathtub, while the child is busy playing and the hair is already wet.

❖ Cleanup after a haircut is easier if you spray a tissue with hair spray and use it to pick up tiny hair clippings.

The Unkindest Cut of All

Few children get through childhood without at least one incident of self-barbering. A quick trip to an understanding professional should repair or disguise most damage.

The More Costly Cut

When home haircutting becomes a struggle between parent and child (or parent and parent), it's time to change tactics and take your child to a barber. Consider going to one who specializes in cutting children's hair, at least for the first time or two, to set a pleasant tone for future haircuts.

It's usually a less intimidating environment.

❖ Prepare for a first professional haircut by letting your child accompany you to a salon whenever you get a haircut. If your child can watch you or a sibling have a haircut, he or she will feel more comfortable with the idea. Remember to take your child only after nap or meal times.

❖ Take two children of similar age to get simultaneous cuts. They'll watch each other and will compete to see who is most "grown-up."

❖ Give your child a bath before arriving at your appointment and arrive with wet hair if your child does not like to be shampooed at a salon.

❖ Let your child sit on your lap in a salon with the cape covering both of you if your child will absolutely not sit in the chair.

❖ Let a child play with the hair clips and the cape as a distraction.

DENTAL CARE

Diet is the first line of defense for good dental care; between-meal snacks and highly sugared foods contribute to decay. Frequent brushings remove the plaque that leads to decay. Brushing after snacks, even healthful ones like raisins or fruit juice, is particularly important. Toddlers and preschoolers, however enthusiastic, need help with toothbrushing; the manual dexterity necessary to thoroughly clean every surface of every tooth doesn't develop until the age of six or seven. To show where plaque collects on your child's teeth and where decay can start, put a drop of food coloring on a cotton swab, and rub it around the teeth and gums. The remaining stains will indicate where to clean.

Dentists recommend that your child's routine dental exams should begin when two or three teeth are in. Some parents take their children to their regular family dentists; others prefer pedodontists, who are specially trained to deal with the anxieties and emotions of youngsters. It is as important for a dentist to watch the shape of a child's mouth and to check the child's bite as it is to check for cavities.

Toothbrushing Routines

❖ Consider cleaning your infant's first tooth or two with a small
   gauze pad, with or without toothpaste. Rub the pad over the
   teeth and gums very gently to remove plaque and food debris.
   You'll probably find it easier to do this with the child's head on
   your lap.

❖ Lie a small child down (on a bed, on your knees) to have better access to those new little teeth.

❖ Let the child practice brushing in the tub, where he or she can
   splatter, drool, and gargle to heart's content.

❖ Let your child perform toothbrushing routines with you, both
   for the company and so you can set an example. Some children are even allowed to brush their parents teeth so they can
   perfect their techniques.

❖ Hang a small mirror at the child's eye level so he or she can
   watch the action.

❖ Get little mouths to open wide for proper brushing by having
   them make noises as their teeth are being brushed: "Hee Hee"
   and "Ha Ha" will allow plenty of room. A Tarzan yell is also
   effective.

❖ Shield your eyes from the "dazzling shine" of teeth well
   brushed!

Maximum Efficiency

❖ To get your child to brush longer and to understand the purpose of it, name every food the child has eaten that day, and
   brush it away. Or encourage your child to open his or her
   mouth when you help with toothbrushing by asking to "find"
   monsters, relatives, and cartoon characters deep in their
   mouth.

❖ See how many faces you both can make while brushing your
   teeth to prolong the process. Keep score while you both continue to brush.

❖ Try using an egg timer, with the rule that brushing continues
   until the sand is down. Or use a kitchen timer set for a specific
   length of time, or for a change, use a music box or a record.

Helpful Aids

❖ Let children use an electric toothbrush if they like the vibration. The cordless kinds are the easiest to handle.

❖ Offer a selection of toothbrushes, in all colors, and one or more toothpastes that the child likes. The small samples or travel sizes are favorites. (You may find that mint flavored toothpastes are too strong for your child's sensitive taste buds.)

❖ Tape half of the hole in a wall-mounted toothbrush holder, so kids' smaller brushes don't fall through.

Tooth Fairy Fun

❖ Get across *early* the idea that the tooth fairy (we had female fairies) pays a whole lot more for a perfect tooth than for a decayed one. In some families, the tooth fairy leaves with the "payment" a note praising the child for good dental habits.

❖ To make losing a tooth more special for little ones, sprinkle or spray glitter on the coins the tooth fairy brings.

❖ When the tooth fairy visits, have her lead the child on a treasure hunt to find what she's left. The first clue should be left where the child left the tooth.

❖ Tell your child that the tooth fairy's wings must be wet in order for her to fly and make her nightly rounds. The child should leave a glass of water on the window sill or nightstand. The next morning the water will have mysteriously changed color from the magic dust that was washed off her wings. (Add food coloring, gelatin, or glitter.)

❖ Perhaps she will leave a note in tiny, tiny writing, praising the toothless one.

❖ Turn a very soft, small doll into the tooth fairy's helper. Sew on a pocket for teeth and money. Or decorate a box.

TOILET TRAINING

While you may wish to choose the time to toilet train your child (spring and summer are the most convenient seasons), be aware that no child will be trained until he or she is ready—perhaps at 24 to 27 months, or even older. Some of the signs of readiness are dry diapers for a couple of hours at a time, the ability to understand simple commands and explanations and to mimic adults at other bathroom routines, an inclination toward tidiness, and a dislike of being wet or soiled.

Remember that if you try to push things you'll only be training yourself to catch your child. Put the whole thing off for a few weeks or months if it doesn't seem to be taking. Relax, and don't pay too much attention to friends' and relatives' advice. By the time your child goes to school, you'll wonder why toilet training seemed like such a big deal.

Basic Training

Help your child understand, once basic training is underway, that toilet habits are his or her own, including cleanups after accidents. Make it clear that this is not a punishment, just a matter of taking care of oneself.

❖   Put the potty chair in the bathroom some months before you think your child will be ready to use it. Explain that when he or she is old enough, it will be there to use. It's okay for your child to sit on it with clothes on to get used to it.

❖   Try letting your child go without bottom clothing altogether, when training starts, to make things easier for you both. (You'll have to be a bit brave to do this, or at least be a good observer!)

❖   Make potty chair cleaning easier for yourself right from the beginning by putting an inch or so of water in the bottom of the pot or place several sheets of toilet tissue in the bottom of the toddler potty before each use for quick cleanup. (Don't keep bleach in the pot. Urine contains ammonia and together these will cause a dangerous chemical reaction.)

❖   Let your child learn by watching you or an older child. Imitation seems to be an especially good way to learn. Or children can learn what's expected by reading books like *Koko Bear's New Potty* (Bantam).

❖   Keep a box of baby wipes in the bathroom for your child to use instead of toilet paper. They are easy for kids to use and help cut down on using too much toilet paper.

❖ Put a potty chair on the floor in the back of the car when traveling, so you can stop along the road instead of having to worry about finding a gas station in a hurry. A little boy can do nicely with an empty coffee can, which can be first half filled with part of an absorbant diaper.

❖ Consider using an incentive chart, with stars or other stickers to mark days or parts of days without accidents, as you may do for other accomplishments. Some parents keep a supply of wrapped small toys in a clear container (where they can be easily seen) to use as daily rewards for successful toileting.

❖ Turn on the faucet and let the water run for a few minutes; sometimes the sound of running water will bring "inspiration."

Using the Big Toilet

Some children are afraid of the big toilet. Explaining the body waste process and showing the child the sewer pipes and other plumbing may help overcome fears.

❖ Let a child who has a potty chair use the big toilet occasionally so he or she can use one comfortably away from home.

❖ Teach a little girl to sit backward on the big toilet (some boys even like this position) or to perch on it sideways. And supply a sturdy foot stool to help children feel more secure.

❖ Be specific in teaching boys to aim before starting to urinate, perhaps by floating a piece of tissue or a Cheerio in the toilet as a target.

Bedwetting

Nighttime wetting, which can continue into the preschool years (and beyond, more often for boys than for girls), is frustrating for child and parent alike. It's wise to check with your doctor to be sure there are no underlying physical causes for it. A recent report indicates that bedwetting can be related to an allergic response to cow's milk. Or it can simply mean that the child is at an age of very sound sleep, during which he or she doesn't read the body's signals. It doesn't have to be just a matter of waiting it out. Diet, behavior modification through alarms, and positive imaging are successful methods to explore. Bedwetting is not a psycho-logical problem, but it is a laundry problem.

❖ Protect the child's mattress and, if necessary, the pillow too, with a zippered plastic cover. Or use a mattress pad with the plastic side down. Place a large towel between the pad and the sheet and you'll need to change and wash only the towel and the sheet. Or slip the old waterproof sheet from the crib, an old plastic tablecloth, an inexpensive shower curtain (cut to size), or a large plastic garbage bag that has been slit between the bottom sheet and the mattress pad. Even a rubber-backed bath rug can be good to use.

❖ Consider making up the child's bed with two sets of bedding, including two rubber sheets, so you need only remove one set in the middle of the night.

❖ Buy large rubbered flannel pads in a fabric store if they're not available in a juvenile department.

❖ Try getting the child up in the night for a trip to the toilet before you retire. This won't cure bedwetting, but it may pre-vent a wet bed.

❖ Restrict fluids during the late afternoon and evening hours, though this will not guarantee dryness.

❖ If you use diapers at night, double-diaper your child. For a larg-er child, you can buy large or youth-size diapers from a local medical supply company. For an up-to-date listing of compa-nies providing large cloth and disposable diapers and under-pads by mail, check in my book, *Toilet Training: A Practical Guide to Daytime and Nighttime Training* (Bantam).

❖ Assure your child that bedwetting for which there is no physi-cal cause will be outgrown, *eventually*.

FIRST AID

The most carefully reared and watched child will sometimes be hurt . . . or uncomfortable . . . or sick. Knowing ahead of time what to do for minor things that don't require a doctor's immediate attention gives par-ents a sense of control that's comforting. A good first aid booklet and a book or two on home medical care are recommended. (The first aid booklet belongs in the bathroom, where you may want it in a hurry.

Protect its cover with clear contact paper.)

Remaining calm yourself will help calm your child in a crisis. Remember that a good venting cry may be the best thing for a hurt child. When you think your child has cried long enough, tell him or her so. The idea is to teach the child that feelings should be expressed, but that there's also a time to regain control.

Handling Ouches

* Make pain time applause time. The whole family can gather to praise bravery under difficult conditions.

* Use a red or other dark-colored washcloth to clean a bloody wound; the blood won't show, and the child will be less scared. Likewise, keep red paper napkins on hand to blot blood before you wash.

* Pin an "ouch" sign on clothes over a sensitive scraped area or injection to alert playmates to be careful. (But be aware that kids older than four or five may find it fun to hit, right there!)

* Paint a funny face or animal with Merthiolate on a small sore area.

* Help a child stop crying by asking him or her to whistle. It's impossible to cry and whistle at the same time.

* Distract and minimize discomfort while your child is getting a shot by bringing along a paper party blower for him or her to use.

* Supply a "pain bell" for a child to ring or a whistle to blow on until treatment has been completed.

* Have a child count while a shot or injection is being given to "see how long it takes," just for distraction.

❖ Coach your child in the relaxing and breathing techniques of prepared childbirth methods to lessen pain. Breathe in time together!

❖ Offer to place a bandage on the place it hurts next time your little one complains of a stomachache. It will help localize the hurt, or it may be all that's needed to cure it.

Bumps and Bruises

Heat or cold . . . which should you use to keep swelling down and speed healing? Cold will help stop the bleeding under the skin that causes black and blue marks, but use it for only twenty-four hours after a bruise occurs. After that, heat, applied five or six times a day for the next few days, will speed recovery. Moderation is the key word. Use nothing too hot or too cold. Don't apply ice cubes directly to tender skin (wrap them in a washcloth), and don't use a high setting on a heating pad.

❖ Keep a supply of ice popsicles in the freezer for pleasurable treatment of a bumped lip.

❖ Try putting the inside of a piece of banana skin on a bruise and cover it with a cool, wet cloth to prevent excessive discoloration. (Particularly good for a black eye and far less expensive than the traditional beefsteak!)

❖ Freeze wet washcloths or water in leak-proof, self-closing freezer bags to apply to lumps, bumps, or minor burns.

❖ Or use a bag of frozen peas or uncooked rice frozen in a tightly closed plastic bag for a flexible compress.

❖ Use a can of frozen juice concentrate as a quick, nondrip frozen compress.

❖ Keep several small, water-filled balloons in the freezer that can be wrapped with a paper towel and applied to bumps to ease pain. Add a little alcohol and they'll mold to "fit."

❖ To make a handy ice pack, fold a paper towel into a three-by-five-inch rectangle, moisten it, and insert it into a sandwich-size self-closing plastic bag. Put the bag in the freezer and leave it there until needed.

❖ Save the old teething rings that used to go into the refrigerator to cool and put them in the freezer. When your child is hurt, the frozen teething ring can be used as a mini ice pack.

❖ Fill small empty bottles (aspirin or pill bottles with childproof caps) with water. Close and freeze. Keep them in the freezer until you need them for bumps or burns.

Bandaging

Probably no item in your medicine chest is as "magical" in its healing properties as a single adhesive bandage. And if one is good, several are even better. Plain ones, decorative ones, or those you decorate yourself or with self-adhesive colored dots all work wonders!

❖ Let your child put an adhesive bandage on the same ouch-spot on a doll so that pain can be shared and thus lessened.

❖ Draw a star or heart on a bandage to improve healing power.

❖ Cover a chafed or scraped knee or elbow with the cutoff top of an old sock to give extra protection to the bandage underneath and yet allow for active movement. A variation of this protection is a terry-cloth tennis wristband.

❖ Make a popsicle stick splint for an injured finger, or slip a small plastic hair roller over the bad finger to protect it from painful knocks.

❖ The next time your child cuts a fingertip or toe, make a bandage that will stay on. Take one of those small square adhesive bandages, and make a diagonal cut at each corner as far in as the gauze pad. Now it will smoothly hug the fingertip or toe.

❖ Put transparent tape over a Band-Aid to hold it in place longer. Actually such tape and a piece of gauze can make an excellent bandage.

❖ Put medicine on the bandage pad, not the sore, when it is necessary to apply something that stings.

❖ Saturate a piece of cotton with baby oil, and rub it over the adhesive part of the bandage for easy removal.

Splinters

❖ Get your supplies arranged before you start: a bright light, perhaps a magnifying glass, and tweezers or a sterile needle. (You can sterilize a needle by holding it in a flame for a few seconds.)

❖ Prepare the splinter area by soaking it in warm water or olive oil, covering it with a wet bandage or a piece of adhesive tape for a few hours, or holding the area over steam (from the mouth of a small bottle of boiling water). Any of these will loosen the splinter.

❖ Paint hard-to-find splinters with Merthiolate or iodine; they'll show up as dark slivers.

❖ Numb the splinter area with ice or a little teething lotion.

❖ Ask your child to look the other way and sing a song, count, or recite something while you prod gently at the splinter with the sterile needle.

❖ Remove a metal splinter easily and painlessly with a magnet.

❖ Use a tweezers to remove any large pieces. Apply a household glue such as Elmer's with a cotton swab to the skin containing any remainders of the splinters. Cover with gauze and let the glue dry. When dry, remove the gauze and glue together. All the splinters should come out.

❖ If you can't get a splinter out, let well enough alone. Most splinters eventually work themselves to the surface. (For one that doesn't, you may want to see your doctor.)

Treating Bites and Stings

In addition to the host of commercial products available to treat bites and stings, many simple household remedies work well.

❖ Rub a bar of wet soap over the bite, or apply toothpaste to it.

❖ Apply a paste of water and meat tenderizer. A paste of baking soda and water applied *immediately* to a bee or wasp sting also reduces pain and swelling.

❖ Cut off the tip of an aloe plant and apply the sap to the bite, or buy aloe gel at a health food store. (It's also good for sunburn.)

❖ Hold ice or ice wrapped in a cloth on the sting area until it's numbed.

❖ Crisscross the swollen area around a mosquito bite with a fingernail (on the theory that one pain will cancel another), and apply some ever-available spit.

❖ Let an itchy child soak in a tub of water to which baking soda or laundry starch has been added. Or go to the beach, just for the sake of getting into the soothing water!

❖ Neutralize the sting of fire ants by applying white vinegar to the bites.

Child Has a Bug in the Ear?

First try taking the child into a dark room and shining a flashlight just outside his or her ear. Insects are often attracted by the light and just crawl out. If that doesn't work, drip a few drops of rubbing alcohol into the ear to kill the bug, then have the child turn his or her ear down and the bug will probably drop out. Never try to get hold of a bug with tweezers or other instruments; you're apt to push the bug farther in, and there's a chance you could rupture the child's eardrum.

IN SICKNESS AND IN HEALTH

We experienced our parents' care when we were sick as children . . . but the job of caring for our own sick children seems awesome. As parents we act as paramedics, comforters, and companions to our sick children. Until your children can *tell* you what is bothering them, these roles can be especially difficult to play.

Many of the ideas in the section Well-Checkup Visits (page 31) apply to the care of toddlers and preschoolers as well as infants.

Taking Temperatures

The rectal temperature is the most accurate. It will be one degree higher than a temperature taken orally. Other methods will give you a "ballpark" temperature if you simply want an indication as to whether a child is running a fever. One is to kiss your child's forehead (the temperature of your lips is more stable than that of your hands). Another is the axillary or armpit method, and another is to use the commercially available forehead strip. It's important to tell your doctor which method you used when you report a temperature.

❖ Make insertion of a rectal thermometer easier by smearing petroleum jelly on it.

❖ Give a child an egg timer or kitchen timer to watch while any temperature is being taken.

❖ Or let the child watch TV or listen to a record, or sing a song together to shorten the wait.

Giving Medication

One of the hardest things about giving medicine to babies and small children is getting it all down. Don't try putting it in a bottle of formula or juice; you won't know how much the baby has received if all the liquid is not taken.

❖ Give a baby liquid medicine in a nipple. (Flush the nipple with a little water for the child to suck to be sure all medication is taken.) Or use an eyedropper, vitamin dropper, or a medicine syringe (without the needle), which you can buy at the drugstore. Squirting (into the cheek area, not down the throat) is easy, there's no mess, and 5 ccs equal one teaspoon.

❖ To give bad-tasting medicine, hold your child's nose until the medicine is swallowed, and then, still holding the nose, have your child chew gum or drink something.

❖ Many of today's good-tasting medicines can be frozen as popsicles, but check with your doctor first!

❖ Ask your physician for the more concentrated medicine. Many antibiotics come in two strengths: 125 milligrams (mg) per 5 milliliters (ml) or about a teaspoon, and 250 mg per 5 ml. If the dose is 250 mg, you'll only have to get your child to swallow a half teaspoon of the more concentrated medicine instead of a whole teaspoon of the less concentrated type.

❖ Chilling liquid medicines can improve the flavor.

❖ Call medicine "the slime" or some equally terrible name to keep a little humor in the process. Most medicines these days are quite tasty, which actually causes safety problems because a child may wish to take more when you're not around.

❖ Get a hollow, graduated medicine spoon from your druggist for dosing older children.

❖ Hold a paper cup under a child's chin when giving liquid medicine. Spills can be mixed with water or fruit juice and drunk from the cup.

❖ Taste the medicine yourself, and tell your child if it will taste bad. If it will, rub an ice cube over the child's tastebuds on the tongue to kill the taste.

❖ Wrap a small child in a bath towel to make physical resistance harder.

❖ If a child absolutely refuses medicine with clamped jaws, gently squeeze his or her nostrils shut. The mouth will open quickly!

Pill Skills and Drills

❖ Butter a pill lightly or coat it with salad oil, and it will go down easily. Or bury it in a spoonful of applesauce.

❖ Place a pill in a teaspoonful of ice cream or whipped cream and it will slide down.

❖ Or press the pill between two spoons to crush it, then mix it with applesauce or jam. Serve it by spoon with a "chaser" of water or juice.

❖ "Give" the pill to the child's favorite stuffed animal first. Or give it during a bath when you can distract your child, and if he or she spits it out, there's no cleanup.

❖ Place a pill on the tongue, and have your child take two gulps of water or juice from a narrow-neck bottle in quick succession. The pill should go down with the second gulp.

❖ Ask your pharmacist for an extra labeled bottle for the medicine your child needs to take. You can put your daytime dosage in it to give to your daycare provider.

❖ Jot down the time and medicine given to your child if you have more than one medication to dispense or more than one child taking more than one medicine. Keep the note posted on the refrigerator. Memory can fail anyone—and often does!

❖ Or make a card to hang on the refrigerator that shows the doses and days. Cross each dose off as you go along to ensure that you give the proper number of doses.

❖ Let your doctor know if your child has not improved within forty-eight hours of taking medicine.

Constipation

Children are as variable in bowel movement patterns as they are in height and weight. Constipation (defined by hardness, not frequency) is best treated by diet: encourage a child to drink lots of water and fruit juice (yes, prune juice); give him or her high-fiber foods such as bran cereal; and give dried fruits as snacks. A doctor should be consulted if a child has great pain in passing stools or if blood appears in stools. Parents whose children sometimes have just a little difficulty have thought up ways to help.

❖   Spread a little petroleum jelly on the child's rectum or on a thermometer which you insert in the child's rectum, as you would to take a temperature.

❖   Sit in the bathroom with your child. Little bottoms don't fit comfortably on adult toilet seats, and moral and physical support helps.

❖   Help your child hold the "cheeks" open to make passage easier.

Diarrhea

Diarrhea can be caused by a number of serious illnesses or allergies; if it continues for several days, your doctor should be consulted. Most often, though, it's just a nuisance and a mess. One worry connected with long-lasting diarrhea is dehydration, for which a doctor should definitely be called. If your child is listless and lethargic and refuses liquids, suspect dehydration. Other symptoms are inability to retain liquids consumed, infrequent urination, dry mouth, few tears when the child cries, fever, and dry skin. One test for dehydration is to pinch a small fold of skin on the back of a child's hand. If it fails to sink back down when released, your child may be dehydrated.

❖   If your child is having a hard time accepting liquids, try giving them to him or her in a tiny glass such as a shot glass.

❖   Serve liquids in a fancy adult glass to make drinking more appealing, but avoid lead crystal.

❖   Encourage a child with diarrhea to drink lots of clear liquids, including broth and carbonated drinks (let them stand for a few minutes or stir to remove bubbles), sugar water, or Gatorade, but *not* milk. Give *only* liquids during severe diarrhea.

❖ Or give Jell-O water. This homemade binder is made by dissolving a three-ounce package of Jell-O in a cup of cold tap water.

❖ Or try water in which rice has been cooked, it's a binder, too.

❖ Don't give a commercial binding product to a child under five or six without consulting your doctor.

Calling the Doctor

Try not to have to hold a crying baby while you call the doctor; neither you nor the doctor will be able to hear very well.

The Heave-ho's

❖ Give ice chips instead of water to a child who can't keep liquids down. A child shouldn't drink after vomiting, but ice chips will help remove the bad taste.

❖ Place a plastic wastebasket on the floor next to the bed of a child who has been vomiting. Or keep a plastic mixing bowl and bath towel by the child's side.

❖ Or spread towels over the child's pillow and blanket; they are easier to remove and launder than bed linens.

❖ For ease of cleanup and to minimize odors, cover upchucks at once with kitty litter or baking soda.

Colds and Flus

❖ Help prevent colds during cold and flu season by putting all the toothbrushes in the dishwasher every few days.

❖ Washing hands frequently is the best way to prevent and combat illness in the cold and flu season.

❖ Teach children how to blow noses by having them close their mouth and pretend to blow out a candle with their nose.

❖ Use a soft, old baby washcloth or a man's large, soft handkerchief instead of a tissue to wipe a tender nose.

❖ Use an electric coffee maker with the lid off if a steamer or vaporizer isn't available when you need one. Be sure to place it where it can't be tipped over.

❖ Or let very hot water run in the shower and sit in the bath-room with the child, with the door closed. (Some people rec-ommend letting cold water run in the shower for croup.)

❖ Hang a wet towel or sheet near a heat source to increase the humidity in a room and make labored breathing easier.

❖ Put a feverish child in a lukewarm tub and let him or her blow bubbles. When the child is bored with that activity, give him or her a popsicle to eat in the tub. It's fun, there's no mess, and the fever comes down.

❖ Coat a much-blown nose with nonmentholated lip balm or petroleum jelly.

Chicken Pox

❖ Give bored kids with chicken pox some paint brushes and calamine lotion, and let them paint the pox marks. It will take them a while to do and will keep them from scratching. Calamine lotion covers quickly and dries fast.

❖ To quell chicken pox itch and other itches, use spray starch (make sure it does not contain sizing) on spots.

❖ Soaking in a bath tub with baking soda also relieves itching.

Coughs and Sore Throats

❖ Elevate the head of the mattress to ease breathing for a child with croup or a bad cough by placing a folded blanket under-neath it. Or raise the head of the bed with a few books under the bed legs.

❖ Make a cough medicine by mixing lemon juice and honey in equal parts. (Do not give honey to babies under one year old; it may contain botulism spores, which is believed to lead to infant botulism.)

❖ Teach a child to gargle by doing it yourself while singing a song, letting the child join in.

Ear Infections

❖ Eliminate or cut down the child's intake of dairy products to help reduce the mucus that contributes to ear infection.

❖ Elevate the head of the mattress to help fluid drain.

❖ If you worry about using a big ear dropper for oil your doctor prescribes, try warming the oil in the small glass vial from a home pregnancy test kit and applying it with the small dropper from the kit. If you can do it while the child is asleep, so much the better.

Sickroom Logistics

❖ Keep medications, paper cups, and other sickroom supplies in a container such as a shoe box, basket, or bread pan to avoid running from room to room.

❖ Or use a lazy Susan for easy access to bedside supplies.

❖ Anchor a shoe bag between the bed mattress and the frame. The pockets, hanging down over the edge, will hold tissues and other small necessities.

❖ Pin a paper bag to the side of the mattress for soiled tissues and other scraps.

❖ Make a table over a child's bed by using an adjustable ironing board, a card table with two legs folded up, or a big cardboard box cut out to fit over the child's legs.

❖ Let a sick child lie on an adjustable chaise lounge from your outdoor furniture set. It allows for a variety of positions and elminates continual propping.

❖ Use a parent's old T-shirt as a sick gown for a child with chicken pox, a rash, poison ivy, or any eruptions that require lotion. The shirt won't bind, and the lotion won't stain bedding or furniture.

❖ Serve tray meals with a damp washcloth or paper towel under the dishes to prevent them from slipping. The towel can be used to clean the patient's hands after eating.

❖ Cover the top blanket with a sheet that can be changed if food or liquid is spilled on it.

Casts on Arms and Legs

❖ Keep a plaster leg or arm cast dry for showering or bathing by covering it with a large plastic bag held in place with waterproof electrical or plastic tape.

❖ Lubricate the edges of a cast with petroleum jelly to prevent chafed skin.

❖ Sprinkle baby powder at the opening of a cast and blow it in with a hair dryer or vacuum cleaner (with airflow reversed) to relieve itching.

❖ Clean up a dirty cast, if you must clean it, with white shoe polish.

❖ Make regular jeans and pants usable over a leg cast by inserting a long zipper in the inseam. When the cast comes off, the zipper can be removed and the seam sewn up.

CHAPTER 4

Coping with Kids at Home

The better organized a household is, the more smoothly it usually runs, but with children around, you have to do plenty of just plain coping with one situation at a time. Nevertheless, there are things you can do to make coping easier.

CHILDPROOFING YOUR HOME

Obviously, there's no way to childproof a house 100%, but for starters get down on the floor on your hands and knees. Crawl through the route your child uses (or will use—you'll want to childproof *before* your child starts moving); grab and pull on everything within your reach.

You'll discover objects just right to swallow, sharp edges on the undersides of furniture, and loads of things that will break off or fall over. Remember too that childproofing (and child-watching!) when you're visiting someone else's home will be *your* responsibility.

The Kitchen Stove

❖ Turn all saucepan handles to the rear of the stove.

❖ Turn on the oven light when the oven's in use and teach children that "light on means hands off." Leave the light on until the oven is cool.

❖ Remove stove knobs, if you can, or tape them so they can't be turned on by children.

❖ Back a high-back chair up to the stove for a young cook, and let him or her stand or kneel on it. The chair back provides a barrier. (You're *right there*, of course.)

❖ Let a child stir food on the stove with a long-handled wooden spoon; wood doesn't transmit heat.

❖ Always set a timer when you're cooking with kids around. Children are distracting, and you can easily forget your food and cause a fire or ruin the food.

Around the Kitchen

❖ Tuck cords safely behind kitchen appliances so kids can't pull the appliances down on themselves.

❖ Use safety locks on drawers and cupboards. Several brands are available in hardware stores. Or you can run a yardstick through some kinds of drawer and cabinet handles or use metal shower rings or blanket clips, at least for a few months.

❖ Or secure kitchen cabinets with bungee cords, pieces of rope, or even a dog collar.

❖ Use wet paper towels or paper napkins to pick up small pieces of broken glass the broom doesn't get, so young crawlers won't cut hands and knees.

❖ Let your child use plastic or paper cups instead of breakable glasses and china mugs. Store plastic cups in a drawer rather than in a cupboard so a child who's able to reach the faucet with a stool will be able to reach them.

❖ Attach a paper cup holder to the side of your refrigerator so kids don't keep using new glasses.

❖ Move all cleaning supplies from that accessible space under the sink (store plastic containers and pans the kids can play with there instead), and lock them up. If you don't use Mr. Yuk stickers, paint the caps of dangerous materials with red nail polish and teach children that *red* means *danger*.

❖ Beware of a child tasting detergent from the soap cup in the dishwasher; add detergent only when you're ready to start the machine.

❖ Prevent smashed toes by keeping shoes on a child who will be pulling cans or heavy objects from a kitchen cupboard.

❖ Don't use tablecloths until your child in the high chair is past the grabbing stage.

The Bathroom

The potential for poisoning in the bathroom is perhaps even greater than in the kitchen. A locking medicine chest is well worth the inconvenience it causes adults. At the very least, create your own "lock" with strips of Velcro. Cleaning supplies, as well as medicines, must be locked up or put out of reach. Consider moving all medicines and cleaning products to a high cupboard in the kitchen where they'll be safer and where children are apt to be more carefully supervised.

While toilet tissue can't be considered dangerous, be aware that for about a year "flushing fascination" may cause waste and perhaps even pipe clogging. Many parents keep toilet tissue off the holder during this period or discourage waste by keeping a rubber band around the roll. It's possible to make a cover for the roll by cutting a five-inch center section from a plastic soda bottle and then cutting a two inch wide slit from top to bottom to fit over the roll. Or, if you squeeze the roll first so it's no  longer round and then put it in the holder, it will be harder for your child to spin.

❖ Make sure grandparents take appropriate precautions with medication bottles when kids visit.

❖ Replace childproof caps on medicine carefully and promptly after use. Save caps from medicine you're through with; they often fit on other bottles or jars you want to keep children from getting into.

❖ Keep the bathroom off limits for a small child by securing a bolt or hook-and-eye screws high up on the outside of the door. Toilets, diaper pails, and five-gallon buckets present drowning hazards in bathrooms. Children have drowned in as little as two inches of water.

❖ Drape a towel over the top of the bathroom door to keep a child from shutting it tightly and locking him or herself in. You can also use a large ball–type ponytail holder placed over the upper and lower sections of the top hinge pin of a door to keep it from closing completely. Or tape the bathroom door latch flush with the side of the door to prevent lock-ins.

❖ And keep handy outside the door the key or a tool with which you can unlock it.

❖ Remove the bathroom doorknob altogether if it's one that doesn't unlock from the outside and you don't want to install another.

❖ Hang three-tiered wire mesh baskets in the bath/shower to hold the shampoo, razors, and so on and to keep them out of toddlers' hands.

❖ Take the phone off the hook or turn on your answering machine while you are bathing your child, so ringing won't tempt you to leave a child alone in the tub.

The Children's Rooms

❖ Use a baby gate to keep your little one out of one room or private area and later to protect your older child's room from a mobile infant or toddler.

❖ Check often for loose eyes on stuffed toys and for parts of other toys that might come off.

❖ Throw out broken toys, for safety's sake.

❖ Use open, stackable cubes or vegetable bins for storing clothes to make access easy for a child and to eliminate the possibility of the child pulling out a drawer on him- or herself.

❖ Secure your child's bureau or heavy bookcase to the wall with hook-and-eye screws to keep a climber from tipping them over.

❖ Glue suction cups or small blocks of cork on the undersides of the corners of a toy chest lid to avoid smashed fingers. Or install a pneumatic door spring (as on screen and storm doors) to make the lid open more easily and close slowly. Better yet, store toys on open shelving.

❖ Don't place a crib or other furniture that can be climbed on near a window.

Graduating to the Big Bed

❖ Let your child start to use a pillow while still in the crib. It helps children learn to center the body while asleep.

❖ Lower the side of the crib and put a stool beside it for a young walker who is about to graduate to a big bed. It's better to help your child climb out safely than to risk a fall.

❖ Push one side of the big bed against the wall for a recent crib graduate. Put a crib mattress on the floor next to the open side to cushion an accidental fall. Or use a removable side rail on that side for a few weeks.

❖ Or start with a regular-size mattress or futon on the floor without a bedframe.

❖ Turn the blanket crosswise, allowing for extra tuck-in along the mattress length.

❖ Roll two blankets and put one under each side of the mattress, lengthwise, to make a small "valley" for the child to sleep in, or place just one blanket along the outside of the bed so the mattress tilts just slightly toward the wall.

❖ Fold crib sheets in half, trim off edges, and stitch up the sides, and your child can keep familiar bed prints in the form of new pillowcases.

❖ Metal bed frames on a regular bed can cause serious injury. Cover exposed frame areas with soft, thick pipe wrap used to insulate pipes in winter.

❖ Consider buying a double bed for your child instead of a twin bed. It makes it easier to lie down together at bedtime, and you can share the bed with a sick child (versus *the reverse*). It also gives more sprawl room. Some parents like trundle beds. A child can sleep on the lower mattress pulled out at bedtime or the pulled out mattress can cushion a fall from the bed. Plus it makes a place for Mom or Dad to sleep with an ill or scared child.

If a Product Causes Injury . . .

Call the U.S. Consumer Product Safety Commission if your child is injured through the use of any product or if you have questions about the safety of any piece of equipment or furniture. In the U.S. call (800) 638-2772 or write: CPSC, Washington, DC 20207.

Doors and Windows

❖ Childproof windows with gratings or heavy screens. In some apartments you can use window brackets that allow windows to open only a few inches.

❖ Open windows from the top if possible.

❖ Put decals at child's eve level on sliding glass doors as reminders that they are glass, not open space.

❖ Attach a bell to a door that a small child can open to give you a warning if he or she wanders out. Christmas ornament bells work well and look attractive.

❖ Fasten an old sock over the doorknob with a rubber band. Adult hands can squeeze hard enough to turn the knob; small hands can't.

❖ Put hook-and-eye screws high up on the outsides of doors to older children's rooms or others you don't want toddlers to go into. (*Caution:* children can be locked *in* by older siblings who are "just playing" or by lazy sitters.) Use the screws also on screen doors, but of course they'll only work in wood, so choose a wooden door instead of a metal one if you have the option.

❖ Attach a flat curtain rod at child's height to a screen door that you *want* a child to be able to push open to keep the child from pushing out the screen.

❖ Keep tots from opening and closing sliding glass doors by placing a spring-loaded curtain rod between the outside frame and the edge of the sliding door.

Stairways

❖ Put up a swinging gate at the top of the stairs; it can be secured when little ones are on the loose and open when you want it that way. A second gate at the bottom can also be a good investment. Never use just a pressure gate at the top, however.

❖ Teach toddlers to crawl downstairs backward ("toesies first") and to get down from furniture backward.

❖ Attach a rope to the lower rung of the stairway bannisters that a child can grasp for help in climbing up and down.

❖ Are your stair railing spools really close enough together so

your child can't fall or climb through them? There are no standard safety regulations for railings.

Electricity

❖ You can simply be sure that furniture is placed in front of every
electrical outlet in your house, but it's better to cover the outlets themselves. Start by covering them with strong, clear tape.
When your child shows interest in removing it, graduate to
pronged plastic caps, available at hardware stores.

❖ Wind up excess length of plugged-in cords and fasten it with
rubber bands or twist ties to keep your child from sucking or
chewing on it and risking a bad mouth burn.

❖ Buy covers that lock plugs into outlets so children can't pull
the plugs out.

All Around the House

❖ Don't assume that squeezing books tightly into a bookcase will
keep a determined toddler from pulling them out. Chances are
the bookcase will topple before the child gives up.

❖ Leave lower bookcase shelves and the shelf under the television stand open for toys and children's books. Your possessions
can be returned to their proper places in a few years.

❖ Cover the pointed tops of expandable gates with old socks so a
toddler won't get scratched on them.

❖ Keep small children and pets from playing in the soil around
your indoor potted plants by buying an inexpensive roll of
nylon screen from the hardware store (or use plastic mesh
squares from craft stores). Cut a circle four to eight inches larger than the diameter of the top of the pot. Cut a slit in the
center and slide the stem throught. You can water through the
screen.

❖ Cover the rods used for handles and pedals of rocking horses
(which are a hazard when kids fall and bump against them)
with the kind of rubber tips you use for chair legs. Or use plastic bike handles with formed grips.

❖ Turn a desk with its drawers to the wall—use only the surface.

❖ Pull chairs up close to the dining table so that a toddler can't
climb up on them.

- ❖ Put the baby in the infant seat *inside* the playpen when you must leave a baby and a toddler in a room alone together. Or put the toddler in the playpen!

- ❖ And put the Christmas tree inside the playpen to keep it out of a toddler's reach.

- ❖ *Don't ever* let a child run with a pencil, popsicle, lollipop stick, or any other such object in his or her mouth. It's dangerous.

- ❖ *Never* leave a plastic bag where a child can play with it. Children could put the bag over their heads and suffocate. Get in the habit of knotting your plastic bags before throwing them away.

- ❖ Cover table legs that need to be protected with pipe insulation. Slit the insulation, wrap legs, and tape together.

- ❖ Pad corners of sharp tables with old shoulder pads. Attach them securely with duct tape. Tell friends it's the latest in shoulder pad fashion!

- ❖ Place an inflated small pool tube around the waist of baby who is just learning to sit to cushion any sideways falls.

- ❖ Remove labels from bibs and clothing that baby can chew and choke on. Even a baby with no teeth can remove them.

Preventing Accidental Poisoning

The most common causes of poisoning in children six and under are, in order, drugs, plants, personal care products, and household cleaners. Children should be supervised especially carefully before meal times— they're more liable to sample foreign substances when they're hungry. Teach your child early to say "ahhh"; you may get a chance to see what's in a mouth and pull it out before harm is done. Careful parents keep the number of their nearest poison control centers posted by every phone in the house.

Parents should keep syrup of ipecac (available from pharmacies without a prescription) on hand to induce vomiting, but use it *only* if directed to do so by the poison center or a doctor. Ipecac is sold in bottles that contain two tablespoons; children under six are given only one tablespoon. The drug's shelf life is five years. Keep an extra bottle on hand that you can take with you when you travel.

SAFETY OUTSIDE

A whole new set of hazards presents itself to a child outdoors and away from home. There are attractive things to taste, unfamiliar settings to investigate, interesting equipment to experiment with, and dangerous streets to cross. There's also the possibility of getting lost.

You might consider attaching a trucker's side-view mirror to an appropriate spot outside your kitchen window to keep a play area in your line of sight when your child first begins to play outside alone.

In the Yard

❖ Glue a rubber bathmat or stick nonslip bathtub strips onto a swing seat to prevent your child from slipping off.

❖ Cover swing chains with sections of garden hose to avoid torn clothes and provide a more comfortable grip. Wrap adhesive or electrical tape over the hose at the level a child should grip, to be sure he or she has the correct balance.

❖ Spread four to six inches of loose material such as sand under the swings and other playground equipment to cushion falls. Dirt can be very hard.

❖ Cover exposed screws and bolts with caps or tape; pinch the ends of S-hooks together with pliers so they can't catch a child's skin or clothing.

❖ Check your own outdoor equipment regularly to make sure it's safe, and also check playground equipment supplied by your apartment or at your local park.

❖ Place an extension ladder across the driveway a few feet from the end to keep preschoolers from riding trikes into the street. Or paint a red stripe across the driveway as a reminder.

In the Car

There is *no safe alternative* to an approved, reliable car restraint—a car seat for a baby or small child under about 40 pounds or age four, or a seat belt for an older child. Parents who are tempted to transport a baby in a car bed or portable crib and to let older children romp in the back of a station wagon are tempting fate. Plus it's illegal. Children usually accept safety habits well if they are established right from the start and *never* varied and if parents and other adults in the car set good examples by always buckling up. To protect your auto upholstery, put a beach towel or a car seat protector over your seats. Also, put a strip of heavy vinyl carpet runner under the car seat.

❖ Teach children an auto safety routine: an adult says, "Hands up—doors closed and locked. Fasten belts. Blast off!" An older child can be appointed "First Mate" to see that the procedure is carried out correctly.

❖ Pull over to the side of the road if there's screaming or fighting in the car. Stay there until everyone settles down.

❖ Spread a light-colored bassinet sheet, towel, or receiving blanket over a car seat in the summer to prevent a hot seat from burning a child's tender skin. When the child is old enough to use a seat belt, keep a towel in the car for the same purpose.

❖ Put a hat on a small child to shield eyes from the sun in the car. Or apply solar film or a car shade to the window on the car seat side of the car.

❖ Transport any sharp or heavy object in the car trunk, not in the passenger area.

❖ Never leave children unattended in a car, and don't leave the

car motor running when children are playing near the car.
Beware of backing-up accidents.

Halloween Safety for the Very Young

This is probably *the* holiday high point of the year! Even little kids get
into the spirit of it early on. It satisfies a need to dress up, pretend, and
party, as well as providing the thrill of getting candy. You can always
limit your child's candy consumption (or just make sure teeth are *really*
well brushed), but don't let that get in the way of enjoying the holiday.

For money-saving Halloween treats, stamp your return address on bag-
gies, and fill them with different kinds of bulk candy. The parents will
know the candy is safe, even if it's unwrapped.

❖ Make sure children's costumes allow them to walk easily.
   Children should wear shoes that fit . . . not your high heels!
   And remember that face makeup is safer than a face mask that
   blocks vision at night. Use masks that block vision for daytime
   school parties. Also, make sure any costume props such as
   weapons are made from flexible materials.

❖ Have your child use a small container so it will look full faster
   and it will be less cumbersome. Plastic bags, plastic pumpkin
   buckets, or even pillowcases will work also.

❖ Put reflecting tape on parts of costumes and any bag or container your child will be carrying.

❖ Provide your child with a flashlight or light stick even though
   you'll be with him or her.

❖ Make sure your child understands that you will check the
   treats before they are eaten. Make sure you've fed your children well before they leave so they are less tempted to sample
   treats before they get home.

GETTING CHORES DONE

B.C. (Before Children), when you could work without interruption, you
may have had the best-kept house in town. That's not possible with little
kids around. "A clean house shows a life misspent" is a slogan you may
wish to adopt. Lower your standards. Pick one or two rooms to keep neat
and keep the kids out of them.

Keeping Kids Out of the Way

You can try to work "around" your kids, stopping when you must and pressing on when you can. You can let them "help" you (remember that sometimes they're really learning!). Or you can try to keep them out of the way entirely by farming them out or hiring a sitter (less expensive than cleaning help, and a good way to check out a new sitter). The cardinal rule for many parents is that naptime and bedtime are not the signals for work to begin, they're for *private time!*

❖ Put your baby in a padded laundry basket or small cardboard box with a few toys so travel with you from room to room as you work is easy. It's a good way for a baby to practice sitting for short periods of time. Or keep your child in a stroller as you move from room to room.

❖ Let the parent who's not doing the housework entertain the child.

❖ Put the baby in a backpack. He or she will be in the desired place (near you), and your hands will be free to work.

❖ When outside doing yard chores, place a child with limited mobility in an empty plastic molded swimming pool.

❖ Keep track of your child while cooking dinner by taking the tray off the high chair and moving the chair to the grown-up table. Cut open grocery bags and tape them to the table as far as your child can reach. Provide crayons, and you'll have time for some no-worry cooking.

❖ Assign your child his or her own kitchen drawer or cupboard stocked with assorted plastic containers, cans, and other safe kitchen items.

❖ Allow your child to play in water in the sink while you work in the kitchen, but do it on the day you plan to wash the floor!

❖ Give a small child a short piece of cellophane or masking tape to play with if you want a few minutes of quiet time to work or talk on the phone. Or put a dab of baby lotion, peanut butter, oil, or whatever else is available on the high chair tray to keep your child busy.

❖ Curb a child's impatience for "the cake to be done" or "playtime with Mom to come" by setting a timer and letting him or her watch it run down.

Encouraging Neatness

❖ Color-code your child's everyday belongings. For instance, your child uses the blue toothbrush, blue towels and washcloths, blue drinking cup, and blue brush. You can even put color-coded stickers or use a colored marker to code other belongings.

❖ Keep a clean, new dustpan in the toy box. A child can scoop up small objects with it.

❖ To make cleaning up a messy room easier for kids, sweep or rake up toys and stuff into the center of the room so there is only one pile. Sometimes one mess is easier to deal with than a scattered mess.

❖ Have a child who gets an allowance pay you a penny for each toy or article of clothing you pick up and store in a big box or bag until payment is collected. Or have him or her do a special chore for the return of a toy.

❖ Or let anything you have to pick up simply *disappear* for a time.

❖ Offer to pick up your child's toys occasionally in return for him or her doing one of your simpler chores. Or simply work along with the child sometimes; it's more fun to work with company than alone.

❖ Encourage picking up right after an activity instead of at the end of the day to make the task less overwhelming.

❖ Have kids visiting friends help with the picking up before they leave.

❖ Help the kids put their things away on open shelving by drawing labels for items and taping them on the proper shelves.

❖ Install a basketball hoop over the kids' laundry hamper to provide an incentive for tossing in soiled clothes.

❖ Keep a tall, narrow plastic container in each child's closet for personal storage of soiled clothes, or hang a colorful pillowcase with loops sewn onto it on the back of a door for laundry.

❖ Provide a visible example of neatness by putting *your* things away, too.

Kids Really Helping

Even very small children can help around the house if you're patient and don't expect perfection. It's important to remember to stress the importance of *all* work, to express appreciation for any job well done, and to switch assignments occasionally to avoid boredom. If you're cheerful at your work and try to find some humor in humdrum activities, the kids will probably follow suit. Rewards inspire help too, and the "house fairy" may visit often to leave treats for good workers. Just be sure to make it a firm rule *never* to redo work a child (or your mate!) has done. Willing help will be hard to come by if you do.

❖ Give a child a card with a smiling face sticker on it to put in a place where he or she has done an unasked chore or favor. Then be sure to notice the card and praise the child.

❖ Try printing titles of jobs on slips of paper when there's a lot to do and you want everyone to pitch in. Include some that say, "Hop on one foot," and, "Eat one cookie." For little kids, you can draw pictures that illustrate such jobs as "feed the dog" and "set the table."

❖ Give a reason for cleaning up and set a deadline: "before Daddy comes home" or "by lunchtime." Not having to do it right away gives a child a choice and makes a job become something to do in a timely manner.

❖ Let the child closest to the floor pick things up and give them to you or to an older child to put away, when picking up is a group project.

❖ Sometimes giving kids a list of things you'd like done works better than nagging to get things done. Or put a wheel chart on the refrigerator.

❖ Encourage your children to help make their own beds starting at age two and a half. By age four, they should be welcome at the breakfast table only if the bed is made.

Making Chores Fun

❖ Assign each child a specific number of items to pick up, and teach counting as the job gets done. Or let the child pick up items whose names begin with letters you call out or that are the colors you name.

❖ When kids want to help mop the kitchen and the mop is too big for them, put two pocket sponges on their feet.

❖ Make dusting or polishing the car more fun by slipping old socks over kids' hands.

❖ Create a "Dust Monster" from an unmatched sock. Decorate it with markers, and use felt circles for eyes, and let your little one help you clean house with it.

❖ Make a game of chores to get children to participate. When setting the table have one child be the waiter and after dinner the other one is the cleanup person. Switch every day.

❖ To encourage a child who is dusting or vacuuming, place pennies in the places that need cleaning up. They'll pick up the coins as they go about their chores.

❖ Put a time limit on chores, or time them with a timer or a record on the stereo to make work seem to have an end. Or have a race to see who can finish a chore first, if the quality of the work isn't really important. Keep track of who does the most, and provide a reward such as being the first to take a turn at a board game.

GETTING ORGANIZED

Saving time, money, and trouble is something most parents want to do. Finding a clever use for an item that's no longer needed for its original purpose . . . protecting a piece of furniture so that it outlasts its expected lifetime . . . making a child's room a haven of comfort and convenience at little or no cost . . . all can give a feeling of accomplishment.

Something Out of Something Else

❖ Use a baby's outgrown plastic bathtub for water play outdoors or indoors, with a big plastic tablecloth under it. Or use it for a portable toy box, indoors or out.

❖ Mend a torn mesh playpen with dental floss or fishing line.

❖ Turn an old piano bench into a play table for children to sit at on low stools or chairs (big ice cream buckets do fine!). It even offers storage space!

❖ Or use an old TV stand or lazy Susan as a stand for a doll house.

❖ Spread out an old window shade on the carpet for a floor cover where children are playing or coloring or creating a toy car track. A flannel-backed vinyl tablecloth works well too.

❖ Use a large old diaper pail as a laundry hamper.

❖ Put small game pieces in self-closing bags. If younger children get into the games there are less pieces to pick up and no chance of choking on the small pieces.

❖ Use plastic travel soap containers to store playing cards.

❖ When your child outgrows his or her baby "squeak" toys, convert them into hand puppets. Cut them off a little below the neck and attach a gathered piece of fabric to the neck.

Kids' Rooms: Walls

❖ Paint a growth chart on the wall or door frame for a visible, long-lasting record.

❖ Cut figures appropriate to a child's age and interests from self-adhesive vinyl. Press them onto a painted wall for economical wallpaper.

❖ Cover a section of a wall with shelf paper for drawing or paint a wall or door with blackboard paint for a child to scribble on. Use a big old powder puff for an eraser. If crayon marks carry over onto a painted wall, remove them with toothpaste on a damp cloth.

❖ Or thumbtack plain oilcloth to the wall. It can be used as a blackboard, it wipes clean, and it's easily replaced when worn. Kids love to draw and paint on artists' canvas too, but it can't be washed clean.

❖ Make a bulletin board from the side of a large furniture or appliance carton. Trim it neatly, and add colorful masking tape or thin molding for a border.

❖ Put cork squares on the inside of the bedroom door. They serve the double purpose of muffling noise and providing bulletin board space.

Kids' Rooms: Furnishings

❖ Note that a low-pile, washable bathroom rug is practical for a small child's room, and indoor-outdoor carpeting makes a good play surface too.

❖ Consider installing track lighting to avoid the problems of lamps that can be overturned.

❖ Suspend a discarded lamp shade from a ceiling light fixture and attach small, no-longer-played-with toys with fine wire or fishing line for a decorative mobile.

❖ Avoid bunk beds, at least until your child is dry all night. It's hard to change linens on both upper and lower bunks. You might wish to encourage the use of sleeping bags instead of sheets and blankets when you do set up the bunks. At least get fitted top sheets as well as bottom ones if you can find them (try a mail-order catalog), or make them if they're not available.

❖ Speed up the chore of making bunk beds by making fitted spreads from regular bedspreads and saving all that tuck-in. Use the extra fabric for pillow shams.

❖ Turn an old twin bed or crib mattress into an extra bed for sleep-over friends. It slides under a bed for storage.

❖ Use bean-bag chairs or big foam pillows in older kids' rooms only. They can serve as building material for forts as well as for sitting and tumbling. You might want to ban shoes in the bean-bag chair. A rip can be disastrous.

❖ Make more space for play and make the room look bigger by removing the closet door and putting the child's bureau inside the closet.

STORING STUFF

The number of *things* a child accumulates seems to be in direct proportion to his or her age. The new baby's clothes and toys take up a lot of space, the toddler's even more.

Another Use for . . . Baby Wipe Containers

- ❖ Store crayons and markers.
- ❖ Store baseball trading cards.
- ❖ Hold recipe cards, photos, receipts, etc.
- ❖ Store baby socks.
- ❖ Store sewing notions, buttons, etc.
- ❖ Store a homemade first aid kit.
- ❖ Slit the top for a piggy bank.

Kids' Clothes

- ❖ Store a small child's socks in the bottom half of foam egg cartons that have been carefully washed and set into drawers as dividers.

- ❖ Store underclothes, socks, T-shirts, and other small items of clothing in stackable plastic bins that are open on the front. They're easier for children to use than heavy bureau drawers.

- ❖ Cut out pictures of clothing items and tape them on the appropriate drawers to help children locate and put away their clothes.

- ❖ Fold a child's clothes in coordinating sets: matching shirt, pants, sweater, and even socks.

Kids' Closet Hangups

- ❖ Make closet lights easy to turn on by tying bright colored spools or old rattles to the pull-chains or cords.

- ❖ Make a clothes rod at child's height with a broom handle attached to the regular rod at each end with sturdy cord. The cord can be shortened to raise the rod as the child grows. Or use commercially made rod extenders, available in notions departments.

❖ Put 12" by 12" by 12" plastic storage boxes near the door. Have your child put shoes in a cubby hole as he or she comes and goes.

❖ Put a low clothes hook on the back of a child's bedroom door for hanging pajamas and robe.

❖ Keep a plastic garbage bag on a hanger in each closet. As clothes are outgrown or no longer worn, place them in the bag. When the time comes for a garage sale or donation, the sorting will already be done.

❖ Use lightweight, ventilated wire shelves and drawers. They're movable, and you can adjust the shelves as your child grows. Kids can see through the wire drawers, which makes chosing clothes easier (and neater)!

Front Closet Hangups

❖ Assign each person a coat hook, and put up wicker bicycle baskets over each to hold caps, gloves, and scarves. Or attach a shoe rack or cloth shoe bag to the wall inside or near the closet to hold winter accessories.

❖ Glue clothespins with a hot glue gun to the inside of a closet door.

❖ Hang your umbrella stroller from a hook in a closet to keep it out of the way, or set it in your umbrella holder or a tall basket near the front door.

Organizing Kids' Toys

Of course the trick is to accumulate the minimum—especially of toys with a million pieces. What you don't have you don't have to store. How simple it sounds!

❖ Remember that horizontal storage is better than vertical for toys; small items get lost and sometimes broken at the bottom of big chests or boxes.

❖ Build shelves of bricks and boards, but not so high that there's danger of their toppling. The area underneath makes a nice "garage" for pull toys and cars, and the shelves are for books and toys.

❖ Put up a wooden pole with pegs, or an expandable metal plant pole, from floor to ceiling. Sew loops on stuffed animals and hang them on the pegs for neatness and decorativeness.

❖ Purchase a package of small plastic rings from the fabric store. Sew them onto the ears of stuffed animals. They can now be hung off the floor on a houseplant pole, but are still within reach of small hands. Or attach strips of Velcro horizontally on walls at child's height and sew or glue other strips on toys. The child "sticks" toys away.

❖ Use a large plastic garbage can (with a lid) as an outdoor toy box. (Also works indoors!)

❖ Or sew old (or new) sheer curtains together to make a see-through toy bag. Add a drawstring through the rod hem.

❖ Attach a hammock to the ceiling in a corner of your child's room. It will hold lots of toys that can be easily reached and grabbed. Or improvise a hammock by folding a sheet or baby blanket into a triangle, tacking one point into the corner and the other two to the walls.

Organizers for Toys

❖ Small suitcases.

❖ A large mailbox.

❖ An old lunch box to store building blocks, little cars and trucks, or doll clothes. Also works as a good portable first aid kit to keep in your car.

❖ The old bassinet.

❖ Laundry bags, hung from wall hooks.

❖ Plastic storage or sweater boxes so children can see what's inside.

❖ Mesh laundry bags. They come with tie or zippered closings.

❖ A plastic wading pool can hold a lot and is shallow enough that digging for favorite toys is easy.

❖ Baskets, attached to the wall.

❖ Fishing tackle boxes.

❖ A rolling wire mesh cart or stackable plastic basket with wheels.

❖ Stackable plastic vegetable bins.

❖ A plastic dish drainer (for books and records; the silverware section will hold pencils and crayons).

❖ A plastic dishpan is perfect for books. It allows a child to flip through them.

❖ Three, five, or seven 46-ounce cans or plastic ice cream buckets, glued together with open ends facing the same way, and spray painted. Set the assembly on its side, like a wine rack, to hold small toys or art materials.

❖ A large plastic garbage can with a swing lid.

❖ Large cardboard ice cream containers.

❖ Large heavy boxes cut down and covered with contact paper or wallpaper.

❖ Disposable diaper boxes and bags.

❖ Draw a picture or cut out a magazine photo of the item to be stored in a box. Tape it to the box so your child can easily see where certain toys should be stored.

Toy Management

❖ Hang a shoe bag in a child's playpen to store small toys. Taking them in and out of the pockets will keep your baby amused.

❖ Buy an inexpensive storage box for your child to store "keep-sakes." Store it under the bed.

❖ Attach a rope handle to a plastic laundry basket, and store a few toys in it. Even a small child can easily pull it from room to room for playing and for quick pickups. (And when your child is through with it, you can use it for your own purposes.) Often they can slide right under the bed.

❖ Encourage the parent of a visiting playmate to bring one or two of the child's favorite toys from home. This allows for trading of toys.

❖ Lay a bedsheet down on the floor to make picking up small pieces of building toys easier. When play is finished, pick up the sheet corners and pour the pieces into the right container.

❖ If your child has more toys than it's possible to play with, put some away for a few months. When you bring them out, put some others away in their place. The toys are like new. Consider dividing toys among several plastic gaskets and rotating them daily.

❖ Make putting toys away a game like "Auction" (you auction off the toys and your child puts them away), or say, "I see something in this room that is blue." The child guesses the toy and then gets to put it away. Or play "Race," with Mom or Dad doing dishes while the kid puts away toys.

❖ Give your child the chance to make a decision to part with a toy on occasion. For a child who tends to hoard belongings, you'll probably have to make the decision yourself.

❖ Label seven boxes or bags with the days of the week. Divide the toys among the boxes and store them in the closet or other convenient place. The child plays with the toys for the appropriate day. You'll have less to pick up, and your child will have "new" toys every day.

❖ Keep a pretty basket or bowl in the kitchen for small toy odds and ends found during the day. They can be sorted at the end of the day and your child knows where to look for small missing parts.

❖ Mark your child's popular toy cars on the bottom with fingernail polish before the toys are taken outside. There will be no question about which car belongs to whom.

Toy Play Tips

❖ Use plastic egg-shaped containers (from pantyhose) to make a colorful children's caterpillar toy. Drill a hole in each end of the egg, and string the containers on yarn. Paint eyes and mouth on the first one.

❖ Make a soft snake toy out of one of Dad's old ties. Stuff it and sew up the ends, making a triangle mouth from one end and adding buttons for eyes.

❖ Add a key ring with a decorative tab to your child's pull toys. It's easier to hold on to.

❖ To prevent the strings on pull toys from getting caught in the wheels, draw the string through a plastic straw or plastic tubing, then knot it to hold the straw in place next to the toy.

❖ Replace a lost round stopper from a piggy bank with an old baby bottle nipple. It has a lip that locks in the hole of the piggy bank just like the original stopper.

❖ Stick tape on carpet to make "roads" for toy cars. Just pull it up and discard when done.

CHAPTER FIVE

The Challenge of Parenting

Perhaps the greatest challenge of parenting is to help our children become social human beings. We want them to become secure . . . competent . . . well-adjusted . . . polite. . . and independent human beings, but those qualities can't be developed by simply following a formula. Our children's unique personalities and our own, plus all the other factors in our particular situations, combine to further complicate the already complicated process of growing up.

MANNERS

Setting a good example in social situations is important. "Do as I say, not as I do," doesn't wash, even with little children. In order to cut down the use of *no* in front of others (and alone at home, too), some parents try to say *yes*, with qualifications. "Yes, you may have a cookie after dinner." "Yes, you may play outdoors after your nap."

Being Quiet
❖ Choose front-row seats at religious services or other gatherings where children are apt to be noisy or fidgety. Knowing they can be seen helps some behave well, and most enjoy being able to see what's going on.

❖ Or sit in back, where you can make a quick getaway if necessary. Some say to exit only when absolutely necessary and to return as soon as potty duty has been accomplished or screaming has stopped.

❖ Seat a child between two adults at a meeting or service.

❖ Teach your children to whisper—a technique that must be learned before you take them to places where talking aloud isn't possible. There's "outside" talking (loud) and "inside" talking (soft).

❖ Find little jobs for children to do when they must be quiet at services or meetings. They can keep track of how many times the rabbi or minister says "God," or they can count the number of children in each row of seats.

❖ Bring an assortment of quiet toys or objects in a small bag for a child to play with at a meeting or service, and let him or her carry them. One possibility is a stack of fabric scraps pinned together. Or take a spool of thread along, and break off short lengths for your child to play with, if he or she is old enough to know not to eat them.

❖ If you need to bring a quiet food, try raisins.

Table Talk

❖ Teach children to modulate their voices by recording them on tape and playing it back so they can hear their own stridency.

❖ Serving dinner by candlelight seems to lower voices. There's nothing wrong with lighting candles nightly!

❖ Set up a series of signals for correcting table manners. Quietly saying, "Twenty-two," for example, is not annoying to children and makes correcting them away from home less obvious. (But some parents say this practice leads to a game for older children, who sometimes enjoy putting their parents through a little exercise in calling numbers.)

The Proper Response

❖ Refuse to respond to "huh?" once you've explained that it's more polite to say, "pardon me?"

❖ Don't let go of an item you're offering your child until you hear "please" or "thank you." And ignore a child who interrupts until he or she says, "exuse me."

❖ Apologize for your own lapses, and ask children to do the same.

Telephone Interruptions

You can minimize phone calls while your child is in the interrupting stage. You can have little talks about manners. You can pace about, maintaining order while you're talking, holding an extra long phone cord above your head. But the interruptions probably won't stop until your child is old enough to make and receive calls and realizes the importance of quiet while someone's on the phone. In the meantime, here are some things you can try.

❖ Take advantage of the time to hold and cuddle your child.

❖ Allow water play in the sink, if you're talking in the kitchen and can keep an eye on the child.

❖ Keep a special box of toys or a pad of paper and a few crayons near the phone, to be played with only while you're talking.

❖ Get your child a toy phone to talk on while you're on your phone.

❖ If you have a redial button on your phone, dial the number your child wishes to call, then hang up and let your child press the redial button, making the phone call by him- or herself!

❖ Teach the child to raise a hand or to place it on his or her head if it's really necessary to interrupt you. You can terminate your conversation or ask the party to hold for a moment while you take care of the child.

❖ Try to help your child know when you *must not* be interrupted. Stand up for uninterruptible calls; sit down for calls when it won't matter.

❖ *Sometimes* (you'll be sorry if you allow it to become a habit!) let the child say hello to your caller, if it's someone like Grandma, who won't mind.

❖ Avoid long phone calls. Reschedule them during naptimes when possible.

❖ Or make your long distance phone calls—you know they'll be short just because your child will quickly demand your attention.

❖ A cordless phone might be the solution to your problems.

Telephone Safety Tips

❖ Pick up your active baby, and take him or her along with you when you leave a room to answer the phone or the doorbell; it takes only a minute for a child to get into trouble.

❖ Hang the phone cord on a cup hook screwed into the wall above the phone so your child can't pull on it.

❖ Hold down contact points on the phone with wide rubber bands to keep a child from disconnecting you or accidentally dialing South Africa.

❖ Place a red dot by the 0 for Operator on the telephone. Be certain your young child knows how to dial 0 and ask for help. When your child is old enough to use the phone responsibly, teach him or her to dial 911 in an emergency.

TANTRUMS

Most parents believe it's best to ignore tantrums whenever possible, because when there's no audience, there's no need to perform. Many caution, though, that it's important not to ignore the child. They ask themselves if they're enforcing too-rigid standards, holding too-high expectations, or perhaps simply not giving enough TLC. Try to avoid the tantrum point: keep your child from becoming overtired or frustrated. Try helping with a toy that won't work, insisting on a short rest, or offering a little snack—any of the three may avert a tantrum that you see coming.

Dealing with Temper Tantrums

❖ Let your child scream to his or her heart's content sometimes (outdoors, perhaps, if you live in the country). Everybody needs to let off steam occasionally.

❖ If your discipline precipitated the tantrum, tell the child firmly that the rule still stands, then ignore the child.

❖ Try to distract the child by doing or saying something unusual or silly. You might even stage your own mock tantrum. Or switch the lights off and on rapidly—another attention-getter.

Some parents say (if you can do this without anger or hostility) to slowly pour a glass of water over a child's head for *real* drama! (Recommended *only* if you are in the kitchen or bathroom.)

❖ Pick your child up and gently shake out the "mads" in a fun fashion.

❖ Disappear! If you're in another room, you'll feel better, and the tantrum will probably be short-lived. If the child follows you, move again.

❖ Ask children to go to their rooms and stay there until the lost "happy face" is found.

❖ Try to stop breath-holding during a tantrum by blowing gently into the child's face, dashing a small amount of cold water on the face, or applying a cold cloth. Don't panic if it continues until your child is cyanotic (turning blue or purple due to lack of oxygen in the blood). If a child faints, that automatically stops breath-holding.

❖ Escort your child calmly to the car or a restroom if a tantrum begins when you're away from home. When the tantrum subsides, return to the business at hand. If you can't leave, simply let the tantrum continue, and grit your teeth. Most of the adults who see it have probably been parents of tantrum tots, too.

Handling Inappropriate Behavior

❖ Whisper, if it's noisy, and your child may stop to listen.

❖ Set a timer, and tell your child that when the bell rings the behavior must stop. Or start counting aloud, being sure the child knows how far you will count. And be prepared to do something at the end of the time; empty threats don't work.

❖ Call out a funny magic phrase ("Un-gah-wah!"), which is *always* your family secret signal to *stop* whatever activity is going on. Remember to use it sometimes in positive situations, such as at street crossings, and be prepared to have it used back to you.

❖ Congratulate your child on his or her control and good sense when the misbehavior stops.

❖ Designate a "time out" place or chair where the child must stay when behavior is out of line, and set a timer for perhaps three to five minutes. (A rule of thumb for time outs is that they should last one minute for each year of age—a four-year-old must sit for four minutes.) This not only ends the behavior; it also gives the child an out, stopping the momentum, which may have gotten out of control. Be prepared to redirect your child's energy and attention into a positive activity when the time out ends.

Calming an Angry Child

❖ Hold a small child tightly; rock and sing. Express your love in terms of increasing largeness: "My love for you is as big as a flower . . . as big as a teacup . . . as big as a bush," and try to get your child involved in thinking up bigger and bigger things.

❖ Whisper in his or her ear. Screaming will usually stop, and if you can think of something really good to whisper, the child's mood may change.

❖ Tell your child there's a smile inside, and if it's not let out, it will turn to a giggle. It often will. Or mimic your child exaggeratedly, and say, "No laughing!" (This, of course, is ignoring the anger, so when it's over, talk about it with your child.)

❖ Scold a piece of furniture or a toy that "causes" the trouble. Your child will probably end up laughing.

❖ Lend your child a hug and a kiss when things are going well; call in the loan when anger strikes. This gives the child a chance to feel warmth and calm down so you can talk about it.

Helping a Child Vent Anger

Children, like adults, shouldn't be required to hold anger in. You may want to talk with your child about anger, encouraging the use of words to express it, and showing your understanding. But remember that doing something physical may be more helpful for the child than anything else.

❖ Encourage your child to vent anger physically by running around outdoors, punching a big batch of play dough, or hitting a tree with a stick.

❖ Teach the child to count to five in a *loud, angry* voice, to play an *angry* song on a musical instrument, or to dance an *angry* dance.

❖ Or shout something loud *with* your child, and let your voices drop . . . drop . . . until there's silence.

❖ Ask an angry child to draw a picture showing the angry feelings—a creative way to relieve them.

❖ Help your child deal with anger by creating a Rage Rock. Pick out a rock together, paint it, then have your child squeeze it when angry. Keep it in a convenient location.

SIBLING RIVALRY

The only sure cure for sibling rivalry is to have only one child; a certain amount of rivalry, jealousy, and squabbling is normal between siblings. It's not possible to make anyone stop feeling certain emotions like hate and the need to win. Growing up knowing that there are times you dislike someone you love is realistic and healthy. It's usually best to let the children work things out themselves, since much fighting is done mainly to prod parents into doing something. Of course, there are times when you must interfere for safety's sake and times when you just can't stand any more fighting!

Fair Is Fair

❖ Be sure your children have rights to their *own* things. It's hard for them to share if they're not secure and guilt-free about ownership. Allow them not to share, if they wish.

❖ Don't label a child "selfish" or show disapproval over unwillingness to share. Make a point of sharing yourself, and be sure your children see you doing it.

❖ Tell a child who doesn't want to share, "When you are finished, Dan may have it." This lets the child know someone's waiting, but eliminates the distress of giving up the toy immediately.

❖ Or set a timer to ring when it's time to exchange toys.

❖ Let one child cut the cake or divide the orange sections and the other get first pick if they're fighting about fairness.

❖ Or assign each child a special day or days (like Monday, Wednesday, Friday) when that child may make certain decisions, select menus, be first at everything.

❖ Play the "stone game": put a small stone in one hand, and the child who picks the right one gets first choice.

❖ Avoid fights over similar objects such as pails, shovels, and balls by assigning a color to each child and always trying to buy those types of items in the assigned colors.

❖ Divide a bedroom shared by squabblers with a bookcase, and divide the closet by painting half one color and the other half another.

❖ If worse comes to worse, hang a sign outside to tell the world your kids are fighting, and take it in as soon as they stop.

Changing the Pace

❖ Suggest a new activity when the kids are squabbling a lot. Boredom often leads to quarrels.

❖ Try distraction when you see that an older child is about to attack a younger one: "Quick, I need you! Please come help me."

❖ Try spraying glass cleaner on the inside and outside of a sliding glass door or low first-floor windows. Put one angry child on each side with a dry cloth. By the time the glass is dry, the kids will be laughing.

❖ End a verbal argument by having kids sing their complaints to each other.

❖ Ask the kids for ideas to solve the problem. Let them think of special ways they can accommodate each other. Even if the ideas aren't workable, the kids will be involved in subsequent action.

❖ Get up and leave the house, if you can, or at least consider the bathroom as a refuge. Like temper tantrums, fighting often stops when there's no audience.

End of Options

❖ Send each of two quarreling children to a different corner of the room, and sit them down facing each other. Tell them they must stay put until they give each other permission to leave. Negotiations usually lead to peace.

❖ Or have children tell each other five nice qualities or actions of the other. Mutual compliments often end the war.

❖ Force a compromise by removing the object of disagreement or separating the children.

KICKING HABITS

Habits that parents don't like aren't necessarily bad ones—more often they're just very annoying. Some are established as responses to frustration or anxiety, others as tension-relievers to provide security in a confusing world. Some parents find that ignoring a habit helps, if no one is being hurt, but others try to get to the bottom of things. Remember, that *you* can't break a child's habit—you can only help the *child* break it.

The Pacifier

❖ Put pickle juice or something else sour or bitter on the pacifier—it won't taste good.

❖ "Lose" the pacifier of a child sixteen months or older. At that age, a child will probably understand the concept of losing things and won't question the fact that the crutch is gone. Suggest that some new baby might appreciate the pacifier now that this child is so grown up.

❖ Start a little hole in the pacifier and enlarge it a bit every few days until the taste and shape are no longer appealing. Or cut the end off so it can't be used.

❖ Tell the child that when this last pacifier is lost or worn out, there will be no more. The advance notice may make the end easier.

❖ Try to coordinate giving up the pacifier with giving up the regular nap, if it's possible. (But remember that if you get the child to give up the pacifier, the nap may go too, whether you like it or not!) A very tired child will go to sleep quickly at night and probably won't miss the pacifier so much.

Thumb Sucking

Many parents say, "Don't try to stop it; thumb sucking fulfills a need for comfort and security and is not necessarily a manifestation of unusual tension or frustration." I'm partial to the mother who said, "Ignore it. Sucking is a basic need. Orthodontia is less expensive than psychiatry." Some dentists feel that if it's continued for a long time (after the age of four), thumb or finger sucking can change the shape of a child's mouth and put permanent teeth out of alignment—a good reason for regular dental checkups. Yet one neighbor told me "My child sucked his thumb but my neighbor's four did not. Who needed braces? All of them!" If you want to see it stopped, there are things to try.

❖ Try giving a baby a pacifier as a substitute. Some dentists say the Nuk pacifier will not ruin tooth alignment.

❖ Try some physical means of stopping the thumb sucking, such as a bad-tasting solution that you buy at the drugstore. (Some parents caution that if a child rubs his or her eyes, the stuff will sting.)

❖ Sew mitts to pajama sleeves, or buy or make finger puppets for the child to wear for sleeping.

❖ Put a kiss in each of your child's hands at bedtime, and tell him or her to hold them closed all night to keep the kisses in.

❖ Restrict thumb sucking for older children to their own rooms. The desire can then be indulged, and you won't have to see it. Chances are that keeping you company in the rest of the house will become more important than the habit.

❖ Ask your dentist to warn the child about possible future dental problems. The voice of a neutral party often carries more weight than that of a parent.

Biting

Children bite for different reasons, usually depending on their ages. Biting isn't motivated by agressive feelings. Those who bite don't intend to hurt any more than a toddler does when shoving and hitting as part of normal play. For a baby, biting may simply be a new tactile experience. Biting for a one- to two-year-old can be a great adult attention-getting device and is usually done out of frustration. Or it can be a way of getting another child to back off from his or her turf. High stress levels and over-powerment by older children can also lead a child to bite. The child who bites in anger or frustration usually outgrows the habit when old enough to verbalize the problems. It's also possible that a child is imitating another biter—human or otherwise. Whatever the cause, vigilance is recommended until the habit is outgrown or "cured." The focus should be on prevention rather than reaction.

❖ Dramatize your pain and sorrow at being bitten; the child's sympathy may rise to the top. (If the child seems to think this is a marvelous game, try another tactic!)

❖ Involve the child in comforting the bitten child (such as applying ice) if you can.

❖ Remove the child from your lap or the room, explaining that biting is not acceptable.

❖ Say, "No biting," while holding the child's jaw on either side of the mouth with thumb and index finger and applying light pressure.

❖ Try giving the child something that *can* be bitten, such as a rubber toy or soft doll. Or an apple or a bagel!

❖ Put the child's arm in his or her mouth and insist on a "self-bite" to show how much it really hurts. Or place your thumb on the child's bottom lip and firmly press down against the teeth saying, "This is what it feels like when you bite."

❖ Say, "Oh, so you want to play the biting game!" if you decide to bite back—gently.

Dawdling

Dawdling is just a form of negativism which most children pick up at age two to three. Be patient—it passes.

❖ Set a timer in a child's room, and make it a game for him or her to be washed and dressed by the time it goes off.

❖ Get your child an alarm clock to help instill a sense of responsibility about getting up. Be lavish with praise when responsibility is shown.

❖ Don't serve breakfast to a child still in pajamas; one who's dressed before eating is ready to go!

❖ Don't turn on the television until the child is dressed, in order to keep distractions to a minimum.

❖ Help your child hurry with reminders of the fun and good things that may happen during the day.

❖ Let a dawdler miss an activity, if that's possible to arrange. Chances are that the child will be ready the next time.

FEARS AND TEARS

The apparent fear that developing babies show by turning away from anyone other than a parent is nothing to apologize for or to worry about—it's a sign of expanding mental and emotional reaction. Toddlers and older children learn fear when they realize that they can't control some things. They may be afraid of being hurt or of pain, or of being abandoned at bedtime or when left with a sitter. Teasing and shaming a fearful child may cause him or her to hide the fear behind belligerence or to give up and become withdrawn. It's important to *listen* carefully to a child to find out exactly what that child is afraid of.

Facing Up to Fears

❖ Reintroduce an eight- or nine-month-old child to the vacuum cleaner, if fear of it develops. Carry the child with you as you vacuum; guide his or her hand to the on-off switch; let the child push with you.

❖ Do something physical about irrational fears of such things as "monsters," say parents who think magical things can only be dealt with magically. Spray them away with a spray can or an atomizer filled with cologne (the child will smell "monster repellant" after you're gone) or just filled with water. Blow them out the window; flush them down the toilet; throw them out in the garbage; have the family pet come in to eat them; or recite a homemade incantation against them before leaving the room. (Some parents disagree. They say that such actions reinforce the fear, because a parent seems to believe in monsters, too. They feel that saying, "There are no monsters, except in make-believe" is better.)

❖ Treat all fears seriously, and do what you can to alleviate them.

For example, if a child is afraid of shadows on the wall caused by outside traffic, take the trouble to move the bed to a "safer" wall or to get an opaque shade.

❖ Rehearse events that scare your child. Play "what if," and discuss what a child should do in case of getting lost, being in an auto accident, or having a parent get sick.

❖ Face up to fear. Admit that you—and all adults—feel afraid sometimes. Tell your child about fears you had as a child and how you overcame them. Or ask the child's grandparents to tell about your fears.

❖ Don't discourage your child if he or she needs a "security blanket" or other favorite object to feel safe.

❖ Hang a picture of a police officer to "patrol" the bedroom at night. You can find images like this at your local school supplies/stationery/educational store.

❖ Have your child draw a picture of what is bothering him or her, or draw a picture yourself of what you think is wrong, and have the child tell you if it is correct. Then change the art, if appropriate, to help change the negative to a positive. Put a smile on the monster, for example.

❖ If your child has bad dreams, turn the pillow over (*good dreams* on this side).

❖ Encourage your child to change "dream channels" in his or her head.

The Security Blanket

Don't let your child think the blanket or other "lovey" he or she becomes attached to is bad. Such security objects help ease the transition to independence and symbolize your child's ability to develop an interest in things outside him- or herself.

❖ Cut a favorite blanket in half as soon as the child becomes attached to it, and whisk the dirty half away for laundering when the child's not around. With luck, the child will never realize there are two blankets.

❖ Try to promote a cloth diaper as the security blanket—one is always available, and it's always clean.

❖ Or cut up one of your old nightgowns into small pieces, if your child has always loved its softness. The pieces won't drag on the floor, and there'll be a good supply of clean ones.

❖ Consider saving the shreds of a security blanket once the child no longer needs it. They've become the base of more than one wedding bouquet!

Fear of the Dark

❖ Take a night walk up and down your block in good weather to teach a child that the dark is magical, not spooky. Or lie on a blanket in your yard or the park, looking at the stars, watching for fireflies, listening to night sounds.

❖ Remember that there's no law that a child can't sleep with the light on. You can provide a night-light easily by replacing the bulb in a regular lamp with a small colored bulb. Or consider a lighted fish tank that the child can watch until asleep.

❖ Put a movement sensor light in the bathroom—it will go on automatically when the child goes to the bathroom at night.

❖ Give the child a wind-up music box, play a tape of soft music, or turn on a radio to distract him or her.

Nightmares

❖ Be sure a child who has had a bad dream or a nightmare is completely awake. Talk to a child soothingly and reassuringly; insist on an answer that shows he or she is not still half asleep.

❖ Take the child to the bathroom; it's probably a good idea anyway, and it will assure complete wakefulness.

❖ Talk just a little about the dream, explaining that it was *only* a dream and not reality. The next day, talk more about it, and discuss the fact that dreams are marvelous experiences over which a person can have control. If something's chasing you, for example, you can turn around and chase *it*.

Fear of Thunder

❖ Play records of marching music to cheer a child afraid of a thunderstorm. The loudness of the music will drown out the thunder, and marching will give him or her something active to do.

❖ BOOM back at thunder.

❖ Or play a game, like seeing if you and the child can sing a whole verse of a song or recite the whole alphabet before the next thunderclap.

❖ Decorate a cardboard "emergency" storage box with magazine photo cutouts of clouds, rain, lightning, and so on. Fill the box with small inexpensive games, puzzles, and markers, and store it in your closet. Take it out only when thunder is heard, and it will shift your child's focus away from the storm.

❖ Say, "Look, God's taking our picture!"

LEAVE-TAKING, WITHOUT TEARS

You shouldn't feel guilty about going out—both parents and children are happier with occasional separations. Children are smart enough to pick up on your guilt and play "poor me." Some parents sneak out while the child is occupied; others say, "*never* do that!" Many do try to leave for only a short period of time when a new sitter is on duty.

Beginning at about the age of six months, little ones cannot understand that separation from a loved one is not permanent. So tears and anxiety are not only normal, but are good signs that a warm and close relationship has developed. The techniques listed below work for sitters, daycare providers, or even grandparents.

For the Very Young

❖ Play "Peek-a-boo" frequently to help a little one understand that you can disappear and still return.

❖ Use distraction to divert a baby's attention away from a parent's departure.

❖ Physical affection by parent and sitter is reassuring.

❖ Leave your child at a sitter's house with a security blanket, book, or favorite toy.

❖ Use a good-bye ritual, including a hug and kiss and such things as waving good-bye from the doorway or window or honking the car horn as you pull away.

❖ Get the sitter to come a half hour or so early so that an activity can be started before you go and the child will be busy.

❖ Spend a few minutes with the child before you leave, and try not to have to rush off hurriedly. This is good for daycare situations as well as when you're on home turf.

❖ Videotape yourself at home doing chores, reading a book, or singing songs so your child can watch you on the tape when you're not there.

Additional Help for Separation Anxiety

❖ Kiss the child's palm and close fingers into a fist, explaining that if there's a need for a kiss, there's one in there, ready and waiting.

❖ Keep family pictures handy so your child can look at them for reassurance. Let your child take a photo to daycare of Mom and/or Dad at work.

❖ Try to be back when you've said you will be, and remind the child that you always come back. Call if you're delayed, and explain the problem to your child in person if he or she is old enough to talk on the phone.

❖ Tell a child who doesn't understand about time that you'll be back "after snack time" instead of "in three hours." For a child who's a little older, set a clock with the time you'll be back so that it can be compared with one that's running. Or send along a clock made from a paper plate showing pick-up time. A child can compare it with the clock on the wall at daycare or preschool.

❖ Forewarn the child about your going, say some parents, even days ahead if possible. Talk about who will be caring for the children and what exciting things they will get to do, but be sure not to promise something that hasn't been arranged in advance with the sitter.

❖ When going on vacation without the kids, give them a sense of when you'll be coming back by filling small paper lunch bags with small treats (coloring book, crayons, and so on) for each day you'll be gone. When the last bag has been opened, they'll know you'll be home that day.

TRANSITION FROM WORKER TO PARENT

Leaving work at work is very hard when you first go back to work. It gets easier over time but usually remains one of the biggest challenges for working parents. Thinking yourself into the proper parenting frame of mind on your way home can help. When possible, grab a piece of private time for yourself.

One of the most difficult parts of working outside the home comes at the end of the day (especially the hard ones) when you switch back into your parenting mode. Listen to a parenting or self-help tape on your way home from work to help set the stage.

❖ Before leaving work, make a list of the things you have to do the next day. That way you won't have to think about them when you're at home.

❖ If you ride a bus, get off before your usual stop so you can get some extra walking time on your way home. Or run some errands before picking up your child or arriving home.

❖ Change from your work clothes to your most comfortable outfit as soon as you arrive home so you can begin to relax.

❖ Make a snack or some appetizers so hunger pangs can be

relieved and you have more time to relax before beginning to prepare dinner.

❖ If a bath is your key to relaxing, take the time to put your baby or small child in the tub with you. It gives you both the chance to unwind and play together.

❖ Can you afford to hire a neighborhood teen daily or once a week for just an hour when you get home to either help with dinner or to play with the kids?

❖ Make an "appointment" for one-on-one time with an older child at a specific time later in the evening so your child is assured of access to you.

❖ Alternate taking care of immediate child care demands with your partner from one day to the next.

DEVELOPING SELF-ESTEEM

Parents who want their children to develop high self-esteem make a point of treating them with respect and courtesy; they don't reserve "please," "thank you," and "I'm sorry" for adults. They don't belittle their children, and they correct or punish them in private when they can, to help their kids save face. And they advise, "Don't take it all too seriously—no single incident will shape your child's character!"

Showing Respect

❖ Knock at your child's closed door, and wait for an invitation to enter. Your child should return the courtesy to you.

❖ Borrow a child's things only after asking, as he or she must before borrowing yours. If you borrow something, give the child an official IOU to make the transaction "legal."

❖ Let your child know very clearly, when necessary, that it is his or her *behavior* that is naughty or rude. Say, "That's a bad way to act," not, "You are a bad child."

❖ Soften a criticism, when you must criticize, by giving your child a compliment before and after it.

❖ Take the time to introduce your children to others, as you do with adults.

Making Children Feel Special By Word

❖ Use your child's name often in conversation and make use of nicknames only if a child really likes them. And use the name in other ways—wooden letters on the wall of the child's room, a sign on the door, a puzzle, a homemade placemat.

❖ Designate a special song for each family member. Making up your own words for variety can make it even more special.

❖ Share a special secret with each child. It could be a "middle child" club, if both parent and child qualify, or a code word that no one else knows.

. . . By Deed

❖ Tape-record your child's voice, as he or she sings, recites, or just converses with you, and play it back for your child, expressing your delight again at these verbal skills.

❖ Keep a running list of positive things your child has done that day on the refrigerator door. Read the list at bedtime to help your child feel good about him- or herself before going to sleep.

❖ Write about your child . . . with your child. Keep a joint diary, let the child draw illustrations, and cover the pages with clear contact paper to preserve them. Sometimes read a page or two to the child at bedtime.

❖ Share baby record books and photo albums with children, so that they can enjoy their own growth and development.

❖ Keep a regular "baby" drawer or box into which you drop an anecdotal record of your child's life several times a year and perhaps even a letter you wrote to the unborn child while you were pregnant. The drawer or box serves as a place to store the child's artwork as he or she grows older, and going through everything once or twice a year is fun for all.

❖ Let the kids entertain you with plays they make up. Give a child a wooden spoon or a single beater from a mixer as a "microphone," and prepare to clap a lot as he or she hams it up!

❖ Create an impression! Cut around your child's hand in cookie dough to make handprint cookies, or make a large hanging picture by tracing an outline of your child's body on brown paper or cardboard and then cutting it out!

Specials for Fathers

In spite of the fact that "dada" is one of the first words a baby learns (often inspired by Mom, who wants to make Dad feel good), fathers often spend comparatively little time with their children when they're small. Today more and more fathers are finding that they want to have a more meaningful influence on their children's lives, and many have developed special things to do.

❖ Take advantage of your natural inclination to get down on the floor and play with your child. Even a new baby will like lying on Dad's chest, and floor play can be a special father–child time.

❖ Share your morning "shave time" with your son or daughter. Make a shaving cream beard on your child's face and have him or her shave it off with a plastic spoon or an old credit card that has been cut into the shape of a razor.

❖ Write down, periodically, your feelings about being a parent and about how you see your children. You'll like looking back on your writings, and so will your children when they are old enough.

❖ Visit your own parent(s) with one child at a time, leaving your spouse and other children at home. It's excellent quality one-on-one time, plus your parent(s) may seldom get to see you, Dad, without your spouse.

❖ Give your time, rather than "things." Write out a list of activities you and your child enjoy sharing, and let your child choose one when a reward is in order.

❖ Remember to bring a memento home from each trip, if you travel, but be aware that it need not be an expensive present. The small soaps, shower caps, and shoecleaning cloths from hotels are always appreciated, as are airline magazines, plastic utensils from meals, and packets of sugar or condiments.

Building Self-Esteem in the Family

❖ Start your day earlier so you and your family will be less stressed. You can also make the mornings easier by getting things ready the night before.

❖ Let each child do something alone with just one parent occasionally.

❖ Say at least one positive, affirming thing to your child every day.

❖ Provide an alternative pleasure for a younger child if an older one has something special planned. For example, if the older one is invited out to spend the night, a little one might be allowed to sleep in the sibling's bed.

❖ Expect your children to do as much as they can, as well as they can, and let them know you do. But let them know that it's OK to make mistakes too, and that mistakes—even Mom's and Dad's—show people ways to learn and improve.

❖ Look for additional creative ideas in my books, *101 Ways to Make Your Child Feel Special* and *101 Ways to Tell Your Child I Love You* (Contemporary Books).

CHAPTER 6

Family Heritage

Giving your child a sense of belonging to a special, important group—a family, large or small—is one of the nicest things you can do. One way of developing this sense is to help the child know all the members of the family and their relationships to one another—not always easy, the way some families are scattered today. Another is to observe family traditions. And then there's keeping track of it all. Even today, with the large number of single parents, family life is possible and necessary. Ex-spouses need encouragement so they don't become ex-parents. Children need all the parents and extended family they can get.

BEING PART OF THE CLAN

Even when family members live nearby, children sometimes get confused about the relationships. Your efforts to give your child a sense of being a part of a clan will help provide a feeling of importance and a clearer self-image.

Understanding Relationships

Who's who? Many families make it a point to discuss family relationships often: "Grandma is my mommy; Uncle Roger is Daddy's brother." And it's both instructive and fun to reminisce about family history and to talk about events currently going on.

❖ Put together a family of dolls or paper dolls to help a child understand relationships.

❖ Draw a family tree on shelf paper or paint one on a wall in your child's room and paste on photos of relatives.

❖ Devise different names for children to call two sets of grandparents in order to help distinguish them—Grandma and Grandpa for one set, for example, and Grammie and Grampie for the other. Or add first names or surnames. Some grandparents choose their own names.

❖ Use pictures to help acquaint children with relatives. Put together an album and look at it together often; give children photo cubes of their own. Or post pictures on the refrigerator or bulletin board.

"Relative" Activities

Nothing can quite replace visits for getting to know one's relatives; if your family is one that enjoys big get-togethers on holidays or occasional huge family reunions, your children are especially lucky. Imaginative use of the telephone, the mail, and the tape recorder can provide good substitutes for visits and gatherings, too.

❖ Let just one child at a time spend the night with grandparents if they live close by. The elders can serve a meal that the child especially likes, and the child can explore the grandparents' house and belongings and learn their routines.

❖ Give grandparents a photo album for pictures of their new grandchild and memorabilia such as first drawings. Ask them to write in the album about their memories. The visiting child will have his or her *own* book to look at over the years.

❖ Post photos of relatives near the phone so that children can see the relative they're talking to. Or make a telephone book for your child, using pictures instead of written names of relatives (and friends) most likely to be called.

❖ Consider joining a "Rent a Grandparent" program through a church, synagogue, or retired people's club if your child rarely sees any relatives.

Keeping Close to Faraway Relatives

❖ Find the homes of faraway relatives on a map. Do a little research on their cities or countries, and ask them to send pictures of their homes, gardens, and neighborhoods.

❖ Or get a large, sturdy U.S. map puzzle, and let a child carry around a piece representing the state a relative lives in.

❖ Let the children send special artwork to grandparents and cousins. Or photocopy your child's hand, and send the handprint with a note to relatives. Your child is apt to get mail back, which will make those family members seem very special.

❖ Encourage faraway grandparents to send notes, cards, and inexpensive gifts by mail, instead of calling. Small children aren't usually able to carry on very interesting telephone conversations.

❖ Let your child add a scribble, a picture, and later, a full signature to your letters to relatives. You can take dictation from the child, too.

❖ Make video and audio tapes, and send them to grandparents and other relatives. Mail the tapes back and forth so you'll have updates from both sides. If a relative doesn't have a VCR, they probably have a friend who does.

❖ Make an activities book for faraway grandparents. Load up the camera and take pictures of the events that make up your child's typical week. Paste the photos into a book, along with samples of handiwork (a picture of the child painting would be accompanied by the painting itself). Have the child dictate and you write on the opposite page. Call it "A Week in My Life," and add a dedication page (dedicated to the grandparents, of course).

TRADITIONS

Some traditions go back generations; others begin when a new family is established and grows. A tradition can be as simple as the daily gathering at the dinner or breakfast table to share the day's events or as complex as a holiday celebration, including special menus and observances.

Beware of inflexibility in traditions. When a tradition is outgrown, store it away in memory, and let it go!

Birthday Specials

Some parents help small children keep track of the time before a birthday by describing it as so many "sleeps" away or by making a paper chain with the child and letting a link be torn off each day. For the little child to whom a year is an eternity, consider having "half birthdays" twice a year. And for the one whose birthday falls near a major holiday, select (with his or her help) another day for the party and some birthday presents.

❖ Join your child for lunch, if he or she is in a daycare facility, and continue the practice when your child is in school. Or let the child have lunch downtown or at work with a parent who works away from home.

❖ Plant a tree, shrub, or perennial plant that the child selects, as a lasting memory of every birthday.

❖ Give your child a gift each year to add to a collection you start in early childhood—coins, shells, stamps, sports cards, small cars, and so on.

❖ Write a birthday letter to your child each year, noting highlights of the year, changes in the family and the child, special accomplishments of the child. The letters will become valuable keepsakes.

❖ Save the newspaper from your child's birthday each year to share at some later date.

❖ Ask the guests at the birthday party or family dinner to autograph the tablecloth with their names and the date; embroider the autographs or have the writers use colored pens. Use the cloth each year, adding new names and repeating the old. Or have guests sign on a white bedsheet, and later make it into a quilt.

❖ Burn a big decorative candle each year at the birthday party for the number of minutes that corresponds to the child's age.

❖ Transfer all the notes you've made over the year into the baby book, put the year's pictures into an album, and share your child's year with him or her. (It forces you to organize, too!)

❖ Select a dull month in which there are no family birthdays, and have an unbirthday party every year, with unbirthday presents for all (unwrapped), an unbirthday cake, games, and songs.

❖ Decorate a tablecloth with your child's handprint on each birthday and date it. Or paint handprints on a wall, fabric, or a pillowcase. It's a great way for the whole family to watch the children grow.

❖ Use the refrigerator and small, colorful letter magnets for celebrating birthdays. Spell out happy birthday, your child's name, and the date with the letters, add a picture of the celebrity, and the sign is complete.

❖ Have children cut their own birthday cake. After the candles are blown out, make dotted lines on the frosting with a plastic fork as a cutting guide.

❖ Take photos of your child on his or her birthday with the number of the birthday written on a large balloon included in the photo. (The date and name can be added, too.)

Gift-Giving Holidays

❖ Begin the gift-giving season by letting the kids go through catalogs, marking items they like. You'll get a feeling for the kinds of things they want.

❖ Take your children to a toy store before gift-giving holidays and let them pick out a toy to give to a less fortunate child, to teach them to enjoy giving as well as receiving.

❖ Have the children wrap gifts in their own artwork.

❖ Use those extra pictures you accumulate of everyone in the family as gift tags.

❖ Give Grandma and Grandpa a toy of the kids' choice on each gift-giving occasion. The toys remain at the grandparents' home, to be played with only there—a permanent entertainment supply for visits.

❖ Let your children wake up Christmas morning with a cherry-red lipstick kiss from "Santa" imprinted on their foreheads.

❖ Give each child a Christmas tree ornament every year; store the ornaments separately, and save them for a treasured collection.

❖ Give your child certain types of gifts every year to make opening presents exciting: something to read, something to eat, something to play with outside, something snuggly to wear, something soft to take to bed. Or just three gifts (as in Christian tradition): something special from Mom and Dad, something the child wants, and something needed.

❖ Take a picture of your child playing with or wearing a gift received from a relative or friend, and send it as a thank-you note to the gift giver.

KEEPING RECORDS

The most important official record that parents must keep is their child's birth certificate. It's important to be sure the certificate is made out correctly and to keep it in a safe place, because you may need it when the child starts school, applies for a license or passport, and so forth. Many parents store one certified copy in a bank safe deposit box and keep others at home for use as needed.

Other records are important for your child's medical history. And still others, in the forms of diaries, tapes, and photos, provide pleasant memories for a lifetime.

Medical and Legal Records

Some parents keep a notebook for each child, combining all medical, legal, and school records. If advice and comments from doctors, dentists, and teachers are included, the notebook can help keep track of any recurring problems a child may have.

❖ Use the back of a copy of your child's birth certificate to record childhood diseases and their dates of occurrence.

❖ Or use recipe file cards for children's medical histories, noting illnesses, dates of vaccinations, and other information. The card can go with the child to camp or school and can be retained for a lifetime record.

❖ Carry a recipe file card in your wallet for each child so that you'll have it to make notes on at the doctor's office; transfer the notes to the child's permanent records at your leisure.

Written Records for Memories

❖ Use a calendar for a baby book if you don't want to keep a regular one. (Or buy a baby record book in calendar format.)

❖ Keep a pad and pencil handy to note milestones passed by your children. They can be entered in the baby books when there's time, and you won't have to depend on your memory.

❖ Keep notebooks of your children's great sayings to read from when they're a little older and to give them when they're grown up.

❖ Start a family diary in a three-ring binder. Add to it as you remember—family jokes, a holiday letter, a record of vacations, and so on.

❖ Mark your child's height on a piece of transparent tape attached to a wall or door frame. Indicate name, date, and inches. At the same time the next year repeat the process, removing last year's marker and saving it in your child's scrapbook.

Spoken Records

Tape recorders are valuable recording tools, even if we do hate hearing our voices on tape. Children usually love recording from the beginning.

❖ Consider taping "talks" that you have with your baby during feeding times. Review the day's events and the baby's progress and accomplishments. Save the tapes for the child to listen to in the future.

❖ Tape-record all kinds of family events, from ordinary dinner table conversations to family conferences and holiday celebrations.

❖ Let your child record a story he or she tells well, at various ages. The changes in voice and vocabulary will amaze you both, and you'll have a precious record of your child's voice, childhood delights, and growth.

Records in Pictures

Get good photos by moving in close to the child and by snapping quickly (babies and little children won't stay still for pictures). Take lots of shots to assure yourself of getting some good ones. Keep backgrounds simple and uncluttered, and get down to the child's eye level.

❖ Tell your child to show you his or her teeth or say, "cookie" to capture that winning smile.

❖ To photograph a restless child, give him or her a piece of transparent tape as a playful distraction. It doesn't show up in the picture.

❖ Have a child hold the family pet or a favorite toy if he or she is embarrassed at picture-taking time.

❖ Photograph or videotape your child getting on the bus on the first day of school.

❖ Take a semiannual picture of your child standing by a familiar piece of furniture or beside a parent whose hand rests on the child's head. Each half-year's growth shows up dramatically.

❖ Make photocopies of your child's hands at intervals.

❖ Trace your child's silhouette from a shadow every year or so.

❖ Share photos less expensively with family members by making color or black and white photocopies.

❖ Photocopy (in black and white) family pictures and staple them together to make a personalized coloring book for your child.

❖ Preserve baby's first shoes by filling them with plaster of paris and later, spraying them with gold, silver, or bronze paint. And take a photo of those shoes for posterity.

Lights, Camera, Action

Video cameras that allow replay on our own TV screens are now so accessible and easy to use that everyone seems to be making family documentaries. If you can't afford to own one, consider renting or borrowing one for special occasions (or just occasionally). Moving pictures capture us in a very special way.

❖ Remember that video cameras record sound along with pictures. Do your directing before you start recording.

❖ You can never pan too slowly.

❖ Short, frequent use of the camera will give you a better history than overly long footage of just a few family events.

❖ No one likes being filmed, but everyone likes looking back on themselves. Knowing this, find a middle ground of assertiveness in your filmmaking.

❖ Sharing videos with long distance relatives is always appreciated.

❖ Consider designating one cassette for each child's birthday, one for special holidays, and so on, and use it only for filming that event. It makes looking back over special events easy to do. And as your children grow up you can give them an annual history, of say, their birthday parties for them to share with their children.

CHAPTER 7

Families on the Go

Today's families are part of a mobile society. They go out to work and play and shop, they travel on vacations, and about 25% of them move every year. Busy parents try to make each trip as enjoyable, convenient, and safe as possible for themselves and the kids.

ERRANDS

Start out with a list of places you're going and things you're going to do to make your trip as efficient and as short as possible. Pile library books, shopping lists, and anything else to be taken along in a special place near the door where you won't forget them.

Shopping with a small child or with several is no easy task. Many parents try to shop alone for big grocery orders, and some say they're able to save sitters' fees because of the careful comparison shopping they're able to do without the kids along. For older children, though, a trip to the store can be a learning experience in both nutrition and economy.

Making Shopping Easier

❖ Get yourself dressed first in cold weather to avoid setting out with an already overheated, fussy baby or toddler.

❖ Keep a few disposable diapers in your car glove compartment . . . just in case. And tuck a packaged towelette and a plastic bag inside each, to make cleanup and disposal easy. Keep extra diapers and towelettes at Grandma's house, too, for unplanned visits.

❖ Hook some large safety pins on your key chain—you might need them for diapers or quick clothing pinups.

❖ Change your baby in the open trunk of the car (with a blanket inside) or on the tailgate of a station wagon, instead of crouching uncomfortably in the backseat.

❖ Use an adult's belt or an elastic stretch belt as a shopping cart safety belt to restrain and support a toddler if the cart doesn't have one.

❖ If your baby is too small to sit in the grocery cart, try sitting him or her in the little carry-along shopping baskets provided. Set the basket in the child seat of the shopping cart.

❖ Keep restless children entertained with a long strip of transparent tape on their finger. If you don't have any in your purse, ask a store worker or cashier for a piece.

❖ Bring toys and a pacifier, to which you have tied yarn or elastic, in your purse or pocket, and attach them securely to the shopping cart. A shower curtain ring works well, too. Stuffed toys can wear cheap cat collars with yarn leashes. (Try this on the high chair, too, so baby can fish for toys—or attach rattles and other small toys to stroller handles in the same way.)

❖ For a teething infant, cover your shopping cart handle with a two-foot length of plastic tubing or a shower rod cover, or make a terry cloth handle wrap with Velcro so you don't have to worry about germs.

❖ Give the kids something to eat, since the sight of food seems to beget a desire for it. Bring a snack or a whole lunch, or buy something nutritious to eat or drink.

❖ To avoid the constant "Can I have this?" questions, give the child one dollar to spend. Deciding what to buy will occupy him or her.

❖ Bring your potty seat in a car trunk even after a child is toilet trained. It may come in handy.

Keeping Tabs on Kids

Don't attach your child's name to clothing in an obvious or clearly visible place, say some parents, since a lost child is apt to respond positively to anyone who knows his or her name, and some strangers are dangerous. In the same vein, avoid clothes or jewelry that would identify your child by name to a stranger. A good alternative is the I.D.™ Me bracelet. You write your child's name and other important information on the underside of the bracelet. It is both waterproof and disposable and excellent protection for wandering children. To receive two bracelets send one dollar and a business-size stamped envelope to: Practical Parenting, Dept. MB-ID, Deephaven, MN 55391.

❖ Ink a design on a helium balloon and attach the balloon to your child's wrist. Teach a child to "pump" it if lost.

❖ Buy two balloons—one for each hand—to keep a child from grabbing and handling things.

❖ Dress a child who's not in a cart in bright-colored clothing (a red hat will do!) to find in a crowd.

❖ Have a special family whistle or tune children can recognize and use to locate you if you get separated in a crowded place.

Involving the Kids in Shopping

❖ Turn your child into a minishopper. Share a handful of box tops or coupons from products to match up with products you intend to buy. Or make up a grocery list in pictures for a child to follow as you follow your own list.

❖ Take advantage of the opportunity to teach your child about nutrition, explaining why you buy some items and not others. Say, "No, because I love you, and I want you to grow up to be strong and healthy."

❖ When you give permission to a child for a major purchase, put the money in an envelope for a week. Then, if the child still wants it, buy it. Interests change in a week, and this helps avoid impulse buying.

City Travel with Kids

❖ Set your baby's infant seat in the baby carriage when he or she is old enough to sit up and see what's to be seen while you walk.

❖ Use a baby harness or toddler wrist leash if your toddler is tired of the stroller. If you embroider it or sew on appliqués, it will look more personalized . . . less like a leash.

❖ Take your toddler's booster chair and put it in the theater seat so he or she can see the screen without being in your lap. A child will be more comfortable, too. And when it's outgrown for home use, store the booster chair in the car trunk for spur-of-the-moment movie outings.

❖ Ride the subway in the front or back of a train, so that the kids can watch the tracks racing by.

❖ Let the children try to guess which stop is theirs so that they will learn their way around.

❖ Or, if they want to, let them sit a few seats away from you and pretend they are traveling alone. It makes them feel grown-up, and they may pay more attention to the route.

TRIPS

Adults may be able to throw a few things into a bag and dash off, but not when the kids are going along. It's easy to travel with a child under six months when he or she takes long naps; with older children, thoughtful advance planning pays off.

Packing

It's hard to travel light with children. Clothing, food, and toys take lots of space, but imaginative packing pays off. A backpack and/or an umbrella stroller are well worth any space they take up. Older children enjoy selecting and packing the things they want to take. You'll need to set some limits as to types, sizes, and number of toys that will be allowed. Take only what fits in your child's backpack.

❖ Invest in a fanny pack (or belt pack) to hold your absolute minimum needs so you'll have both hands available for your child and you won't have to carry a purse.

❖ Simplify dressing for the whole family by designating specific bags for specific items: "Susie's clothes," for example, or a nighttime suitcase for the whole family. Put children's clothing on top for easy access if you're sharing suitcases.

❖ Use duffel bags for kids' clothes and toys—they'll fit more easily into the car or trunk. A nylon duffel bag can be used for wet or soiled diapers. It can be washed if needed and reused. It's also good for wet clothes and bathing suits.

❖ Save space by bringing inflatable toys. When not in use, they can be deflated and tucked away.

❖ Pack disposable diapers in the corners of suitcases to save the space a big bag or box will take.

❖ Let the baby's quilt double as a changing pad if you're taking it along. Slip it in a pillowcase and tie a ribbon around it for easy carrying.

❖ Pack several large plastic bags. They can be used under sheets for the occasional bedwetter and for soiled laundry. Or bring a bath rug with rubber backing to lay down on top of the sheet. They roll up easily for travel.

❖ Use a see-through lingerie case with zipper pockets and a hanger for small items for babies and parents. The bag is easily moved and hung, and the contents are visible.

❖ Bring along your baby's room monitor. It can be helpful whether at Grandma's or in a hotel to monitor a waking baby who is out of earshot.

❖ Take along a night-light to reassure children waking in the night in a strange room.

❖ Pack a few of the baby's things that will make strange surroundings seem more like home—a crib sheet or receiving blanket that you use in the crib at home, a toy or two usually kept in the crib, and a plexiglass mirror to put in the new crib so the baby can see him- or herself when waking up.

❖ Take along a few electrical outlet covers as a traveling child-proofing measure if you'll be staying at a hotel or in the homes of others who might not have them.

❖ Tag special pillows, blankets, and toys with your name and address so they can be returned if left somewhere.

❖ Keep plastic bandages and baby wipes in the glove compartment of the car, or in a purse, pocket, or carry-on bag if you're traveling by plane. Be sure you have medication packed with you and not in your luggage. Keep your M.D. and pharmacy phone numbers with you . . . just in case.

Comfort in the Car

Even if you travel in a large car, van, or station wagon with plenty of room, you'll want to organize things so that they'll be easy to get at and not cause clutter.

❖ Make a slipcover for the front seat of the car with several pockets stitched to the side that will hang over the back for books, games, and toys. A shoe bag (with many pockets) is pefect for organizing all your travel "stuff."

❖ Stuff a pillowcase with bulky cold-weather clothing. You'll have a pillow for napping, and the clothing will be in one place.

❖ Consider renting at your destination a playpen or other needed equipment you can't take along. Diaper services, too!

Peace in the Car

Parents who travel a lot are used to children's initial excitement and restlessness in the car. The kids usually settle in after an hour or so, once territories and rules have been set. Don't start the car until everyone's buckled. If a child unbuckles while you're driving, pull off to the side and sadly say, "Oh dear, the car won't go unless your seat belt is buckled." Traveling with kids just takes longer. Build that into your travel schedule.

For a Fussy Traveler

❖ Bring out a new toy or snack periodically.
❖ Keep the radio on with lively music.
❖ Sing lots of songs.
❖ Keep trips very short if your child's an unhappy camper.
❖ Stop every hour or two.
❖ Praise positive behavior.

❖ Travel at night, or get a very early start, so that the children will sleep in the car, but don't encourage so much sleep that you'll have well-rested, active kids at night when you're ready to rest.

❖ Put a small suitcase or box between two children in the back-seat to clearly separate sides. Or place a firm-sided diaper bag filled with small toys and books between two toddlers in car seats. It can be reached easily by the children and holds enough to keep them busy for quite a distance. (Stash some of the children's favorite toys and books in the bag well in advance of a trip so they will have more appeal.)

❖ Make seating arrangements changeable. One adult in the back seat for all or half of a trip usually makes for pleasant riding.

❖ Stop often to run and play with the kids. You all need the break. Pack a bottle of bubbles or a package of balloons into the glove compartment. Keep a frisbee, ball, and a jump rope stashed under the car seat, too. When it's time for a stop, your child will have several ways to happily burn off some energy.

❖ Give the kids a five-minute warning before you stop so that they can put on shoes and sweaters or coats.

❖ Plan and announce a treat for the end of the day, so everyone will have something to look forward to: a swim in a motel pool, dinner at a restaurant, a pop stop.

❖ Take along earphones for kids—and earplugs for the adults!

Food in the Car

If you carry an extra set of clothing for each child and a plastic bag for soiled clothes, a spill or an accident won't be a disaster. It's also a good idea to cover the backseat with a sheet or cotton blanket; you can shake out the crumbs at rest stops. Keep baby wipes or packaged towelettes handy, and bring along a squeeze bottle of water with a little liquid soap added. You can always use the spray from the windshield wipers to clean up your car as a last resort.

❖ Use an insulated six-pack bag to keep baby food warm or cold. Tape the baby spoon to one of the jars.

❖ Fill a small plastic jar with water, two to three drops of liquid soap, and a washcloth for a handy wet cloth to clean up spills or dirty faces.

❖ Use a cardboard six-pack carton when traveling. Each compartment will hold a little sack of pretzels, candy, napkins, or juice. It's easy to carry.

❖ See pages 7–9 for ideas about baby bottles.

❖ Pack instant baby cereal in separate small plastic bags or containers with powdered milk or formula, and add warm water from a thermos or the hot tap of a sink when you're ready to feed the baby. Carry frozen baby food cubes or "plops" for babies and your own juice popsicles for older kids in a freezer chest.

❖ Carry a supply of small paper plates or coffee filters with little slits in the center. Put the sticks of popsicles or ice cream bars through the slits, and there'll be less mess on car seats and fingers.

❖ Hang a bagel for munching on a string tied around the car seat handle. There won't be many crumbs, and it won't fall on the floor.

❖ Cut sandwiches in different shapes for easy identification: triangles for those with mustard, rectangles for those with mayonnaise, for example.

❖ Fill several small plastic bags with an assortment of such treats as raisins, dry cereal, and sunflower seeds, and bring them out when spirits need reviving.

❖ Take along a box of crackers and a tube of squirt cheese. The adult who's not driving can decorate the crackers with the cheese in designs, letters, or numbers.

❖ Avoid taking very salty foods in the car—they call for lots of drinking and then for stops at restrooms.

Drinks in the Car

❖ Carry a thermos of cold water—it quenches thirst best. Add a little lemon juice for flavor.

❖ Hang canteens or wineskins filled with water or juice from the garment hook on each side of the back seat so children can serve themselves.

❖ Make crisscross slits in a baby bottle nipple; invert and secure it with the cap and cover on a plastic baby bottle filled with your toddler's favorite drink. Remove the cover and insert a straw when he or she wants a drink—no spills!

❖ Or put the liquids in well-washed plastic lemon or lime juice dispensers. (Remove the inserts with a sharp pointed object, replace after filling and screw the caps back on.) If you freeze them before you leave, the drinks will stay cool as they melt.

❖ Satisfy both thirst and hunger with grapes. Oranges serve the same purpose, but they're messier.

❖ Freeze a large or small half-full plastic container of water. When you're ready to go, fill the balance of the container with water for a long-lasting, cold thirst quencher.

❖ Don't forget to take a cloth diaper or two to mop up spills— they're very absorbent.

❖ Keep flexible straws in your purse. They make it easier for children in a restaurant or car seat to drink from cups.

❖ Buy some plastic drink box holders to prevent the inevitable squeezes and squirts that occur with regular juice boxes.

❖ Carry a collapsible cup for the child too old for a bottle but too small to reach a drinking fountain. Clean tops from large detergent bottles can act as disposable cups. Clean yogurt cups work well, too.

❖ Give your child a plastic bottle with straw (the kind used by bicyclists) for a nonspillable drink.

❖ Refill pint-size plastic juice bottles from the grocer's fresh-squeezed juice bar with water or juice. They're great for taking on short outings, and they save the cost of small boxed drinks.

Eating in Restaurants

❖ Assemble your own "restaurant kit" with children's utensils, snacks, baby wipes, a high chair strap or belt, small toys, and a small plastic clothespin, diaper pin, or sweater guard to snap a napkin around a child's neck (better yet, a bib or two!). Make restaurant personnel happy by bringing a piece of newspaper to spread out under the high chair. Bring a cheap and easy booster seat: a couple of old catalogs wrapped in contact paper or duct tape.

❖ Let kids drink with straws—they're fun, and they help prevent spills. Cutting them down or in half makes handling easier.

❖ Get in the habit of always carrying small pads of paper and colored pencils in your bag. They come in handy at restaurants, doctors' offices, and other places where you must wait.

❖ Ask an attendant for a take-out cup with a lid. Put a straw through the slit and with luck you'll eliminate spills from glasses in restaurants.

❖ Let someone walk around outdoors with an impatient toddler while you're waiting for the food to be served. Or let the child play with (not eat) ice cubes on the high chair tray, or with paper napkins or straws.

❖ Order food with take-out potential. And ask the server which dishes take the least amount of time to get to the table.

❖ Order a pot of hot water and extra napkins for cleanup and, perhaps, to wash a high chair tray that's not quite clean.

Toys to Take Along

❖ Before embarking on a long car trip, wrap a variety of small personalized gifts for your child. Have him or her open the gifts at predetermined times. Be careful not to buy gifts that would be too noisy in a car (whistles) or messy (paint by numbers). The purpose is to occupy the child immediately.

❖ Bring a plastic dishpan to hold your tot's favorite toys and books. Set it beside his or her car seat for a self-service library.

❖ Buckle your child's favorite stuffed animal in your child's empty car seat. It will always be there to play with in the car, plus it sets a good example.

❖ Keep the toy supply in the trunk, and bring out a few items after every rest stop, for variety, returning those in the car to the trunk.

❖ Tie toys to a child's car seat with short strings so that you won't have to pick them up constantly.

❖ Let the children fill school lunch boxes with small toys to play with but not *so* small that they can get lost in the car.

❖ Put tiny toys that must go along in a shoe bag (closet-organizer). Keep it rolled up in the car; let it hang on a hotel room door.

❖ Wrap some favorite toys and new little surprises with plenty of string and tape. Unwrapping time will give you some peace, though you'll have some litter to clean out of the car.

Activities in the Car

Check at your local library for books on games to play and songs to sing in the car. Keep a list of favorite songs and games in the glove compartment so you won't forget them when you suddenly need diversion.

❖ Tape greeting cards, pictures from magazines, even a swatch of a baby's wallpaper to the back of the front seat, so the back car-seat rider will have something interesting to look at.

❖ Draw faces on your child's fingers or hands (or on your own) with washable marker to make puppet conversations or stories.

❖ Make a simple map even small children can follow as you drive in the car, with stops you're sure of marked.

❖ Put everyone's imagination to the test by "seeing things" in cloud formations.

❖ Store colored pencils, markers, and coloring books in a metal cake pan with a sliding cover (crayons melt in the summer heat). The closed top provides a work surface. Avoid scissors— their sharp points may prove dangerous in case of a sudden stop.

❖ Buy magnetized games, or glue pieces of Velcro on board games and their playing pieces to keep small parts from getting lost. For a dice game, put dice in a clear plastic jar so that you can just shake them, rather than roll and risk losing them.

❖ Take along a big catalog for the children to look at.

❖ Buy a small photo album and fill it with pictures of friends and family to amuse children in a car. Keep updating it.

❖ Purchase postcards of favorite sites when traveling. Write down the day's activities on the back of the cards. Put them in a scrapbook you've brought along or mail them to your home address.

❖ Play tapes you've made of favorite stories and songs, or use tapes you've checked out from the library.

Traveling by Plane

Babies under two travel free, but you must inform the airline that you are traveling with an infant. Check with the airlines or a travel agent to determine the days of the week and the hours of flights that are least crowded so that you might be able to get an extra seat for the baby. (Remember that the trick of traveling at night by car, so the kids will sleep, doesn't necessarily transfer to air travel.)

❖ Request the window and aisle seats in a three-row section and hope that the middle seat won't be taken.

❖ Try to board the plane with a freshly diapered baby. There's little room for changing in an airplane restroom. Double-diapering is best. Carry a soft cloth diaper bag with a shoulder strap or a backpack instead of a bulkier "boxy" bag. Fill it with more diapers than you think you will need, in case of the unexpected. Motion sickness bags are good for soiled diapers but don't leave them filled at your seat.

❖ Board early when you can. Get a blanket and pillow from the overhead rack as you are being seated.

❖ Carry a small infant in a front pack to avoid his or her slipping out of your arms and to free your hands while asleep. Some feel

the front pack is safest for takeoff and landing. Make sure the
seat belt is over *your* pelvis, not the baby's.

❖ Nurse your baby or give a bottle or pacifier at takeoff and landing to reduce pressure on ears. Have gum or hard candy available for older children. Blowing up a balloon often helps older
children, too. Teach children to swallow, chew, and yawn to
open eustachian tubes. Make a game of facial motions for your
baby. Even the crying some children do when their ears hurt
helps equalize pressure imbalance. This is especially important
if a child has a cold or allergies.

❖ Most car seats can now be taken on board an airplane. Check
with your airline to make sure yours is an approved model.
Remember that you'll be paying for another seat if your child is
under two and you want to be assured of an extra seat.

❖ Let a child old enough to do so carry his or her own things in a
backpack.

❖ Bring a few new, small toys and books and hand them out one
at a time. A deck of cards is good. Be sure not to bring anything that could be dangerous if your child were to throw it.

❖ As you leave the plane, don't rush. Seasoned air travelers say
leaving last is best with kids unless you're right up front.

Eating on the Plane

❖ Request a child's plate or fruit plate at least two days before
departing to get more appropriate finger foods.

❖ Check with a flight attendant to find the best time to get his
or her help with warming food or feeding a baby.

❖ Bring some food from home for your child. Airplane snacks are
often nuts or crunchy things babies shouldn't eat, and you'll
have something in case of delays. Cheerios are a good no-
crumb snack.

❖ Avoid cola drinks for children. Two or three have as much caffeine as a cup of coffee, and they'll make it hard for a child to
sit still. They're also diuretic.

❖ Don't drink hot beverages while your child is active or in your
lap; if they spill, your child may be scalded.

ENJOYING THE OUTDOORS

It's important to remember that children, even responsible preschoolers, must be watched constantly and extra carefully when you're in the woods or near water. Possibilities for fun and learning are there, however. Rainy-day puddles are as exciting as sunsets and wildlife.

Camping with Kids

Roughing it with small children is not for everyone; if you're not sure you can take it, choose a campground with bathrooms, laundry facilities, and a general store for your first outing. You may feel safer if your campsite is not near a road, lake, or stream. As with any trip, accept each moment for its own enjoyment—original plans and destinations sometimes have to be modified.

Before the Camping Trip

❖ Stage a practice run in your backyard. You can test all your equipment and accustom your child to the experience.

❖ Include rain gear, boots, and jackets when packing, no matter what the weather report says. Make washability a priority for camping clothes, and keep layering in mind when selecting them.

❖ Pack some clothing and gear in plastic pails of various sizes that you can use for dishwashing, hand laundry, and grooming. A large plastic container with a lid makes a great mini laundry tub for little items. Just add a little soap, put on the lid, and shake. Shaking is more efficient than swishing in a pail.

❖ Avoid the odors of damp, soiled clothing by packing fabric softener sheets in laundry bags.

❖ Take along a backpack carrier so that you can carry a young child, but build up your carrying time before your trip. And pack a small mirror that you can use as a rear view mirror while you're hiking.

❖ Make up a nature box, including books on birds, rocks, and trees and plenty of plastic bags, jars, and boxes to hold collections. Give your child collecting assignments: three leaves, five rocks, two pinecones.

❖ Pack a first aid book and a good first aid kit, including supplies for hazards like insects, sun, cuts and bruises, and fever. Include a tweezers for the splinters that someone's sure to pick up.

❖ Consider taking along your own drinking water, if you don't trust the water at the campground. You *don't* want your child to get diarrhea!

On the Camping Trip

❖ Use empty plastic bread bags for soiled diapers and other wet items.

❖ Use your empty cooler as a quick bathtub. (Never leave your child alone near even this water!)

❖ Or use a small inflatable wading pool for a child's bathtub. You can add a quilt or pad and use it as a crib or playpen, too.

❖ Travel with food and drink in the car at all times, even if you plan to buy most supplies at your campground, so that you're prepared for anything.

❖ Create a nature bracelet by putting a loose strip of transparent tape around children's wrists, sticky side up. Small nature treasures can be stuck to their nature bracelet when out hiking and exploring.

❖ Keep Avon's Skin-So-Soft towelettes in your baby bag to use whenever mosquitoes start biting. (Canned spray repellants should not be used on babies.)

At the Beach

❖ Remember that children burn much more easily than adults. Put hats on small children, and use a good sun block on their skin. Don't spray lotion on children. Spray it on your hand, and then apply it to a child's face.

❖ Use a big sheet for children to sit on instead of a blanket or towel. It's cooler, sand will shake off easily, and it will fold neatly and compactly for storage.

❖ Put beach gear, if there's a lot of it, into a plastic sled or laundry basket to pull across the sand.

❖ Or carry beach toys in a plastic laundry basket or mesh bag that you can dunk in the water for a quick rinse and drain at the end of the day.

❖ Prop up a baby at the beach in a plastic laundry basket lined with towels to keep him or her safe and out of the sand.

❖ Use a round toothbrush holder to carry a paring knife or baby food spoon when traveling to a picnic or to the beach.

❖ Mark your beach toys. Yours will probably look like everyone else's. Red nail polish works well.

❖ Put large jar lids under the legs of a playpen, if you set it up at the beach, to keep them from sinking into the sand. (This works well in your yard at home, too.)

❖ Turn a playpen upside down over a blanket or sheet to keep the hot sun off a child and the child off the hot sand. Or open a large umbrella on a blanket.

❖ Remove diapers when giving a baby a swim. They absorb too much water and become very heavy so that the baby loses natural buoyancy.

❖ Fill a child's pail with water when leaving the beach, and have the children dip their feet in it before entering the car.

❖ Or dust baby powder over children's sandy, dry arms and legs. Brush off powder and sand together.

❖ To remove sand from chairs, buckets, shovels, and even feet, use a clean, broad paint brush you keep in your car trunk.

❖ Remove sand and dirt from pant cuffs with the sweeper attachment of your vacuum cleaner.

MOVING

Parents who have moved a lot say they try not to let a move disrupt their children's sense of security. You can help make the transition easier by involving your children as much as possible, letting them be the first to know about the move, and sharing your enthusiasm and excitement with them.

Before You Move

❖ If it's an in-town move, take the children to see the new house or apartment, at least from the outside. Show them the points of interest in the neighborhood. If possible, let them meet and talk with any children who live in your future home or neighborhood. If you're moving out of town, try to get photos of the new home and local landmarks.

❖ Spend some relaxed family time in the new home before the move, if you can. Hang a few pictures and bring in some familiar small objects and toys to bridge the gap between old and new.

❖ If some of the children's things will be sold, let them decide which they will be; if possible, earmark the money from them for new toys in the new home.

❖ Let the kids pack their possessions as you pack yours, to give them the feeling of helping. Let them decorate their own boxes, and they'll know which things they want to see unpacked first.

❖ Give yourself a break and save time and work by having a sitter play with the kids while you do the packing.

❖ Pack two sheets and a blanket in the box that holds each mattress so that you can be assured of ready beds amid all the unpacking.

❖ Load children's furniture and boxes last, so that they will be first off.

The New Environment

The day or days of moving out of one home and into another can be traumatic for both children and adults, but they can also be fun and exciting. Some parents believe it's best to have the kids out of the house at both ends of a move, if possible, dismantling their old rooms and setting up the new ones while the kids are gone. Other parents recommend involving the children throughout the move, doing everything as a family.

❖ Nurse a baby through your move and plan to wean only after you are settled. And hope you are not in the middle of toilet training during a move.

❖ Set up a child's room first.

❖ Find a sitter at your new location, if you can, to play with the children while you unpack. Besides being able to settle in more easily, you'll have a chance to observe and supervise the new sitter.

❖ Have a picnic in the new house for the first meal, with favorite easy foods or sandwiches. Make it special, amid the confusion and disarray. Talk about how things will be in a week . . . or a month . . . and remind the kids that they may never be able to eat in the center of the dining room floor again.

❖ Pay kids a penny (or a nickel or quarter) for each moving sticker they remove from furniture.

❖ Ask a friend or relative to send your child a welcoming postcard or letter to the new address, so that it will be waiting when you get there.

CHAPTER 8

Child's Play

Child's play is learning, and many who have studied child development say that the more imaginative the play, the more a child will learn. Most parents have seen a child become more fascinated with the box a toy comes in than with the toy itself. This is not to say that you shouldn't buy toys, but to suggest that the fun and learning of play can depend upon what's at hand as well.

SEASONAL FUN

A climate like that of the South Sea Islands often seems like a dream come true to parents of active kids: warm weather, year 'round . . . no mittens, caps, scarves, jackets. Hardy souls in the north, though, enjoy the change between summer and winter activities.

Warm Weather Specials

- ❖ Attach a special baby swing to the older children's swing set so that all the kids can swing together.
- ❖ Put an old rubber doormat or a piece of indoor–outdoor carpeting under the swing to protect shoes and to keep some of the dirt outdoors.

❖ Fill a flour shaker with cornstarch or flour, and let the kids sprinkle everything in sight outdoors. The first shower will clean it all up.

❖ Let the kids draw on the sidewalk with white or colored chalk. Rain or a hose will erase the artwork.

❖ Make a sandbox by setting an old tractor tire on the ground and filling it about half full of sand—there's plenty of seating space all around. Or use an old plastic swimming pool that will no longer hold water. Sink it into the ground, punch a few holes in the bottom, and fill it with sand—the coarse kind, not the fine variety. Or don't bother to sink it. As an alternative to sand, fill it with a large bag or two of bird seed (assuming your child is old enough to know not to eat it). Add shovels, toys, and a child for a fun afternoon.

❖ Hang blankets over the clothesline to make a tent. Or set up a real tent for outdoor sleepovers or naps.

❖ Invert a plastic wading pool over your sandbox to protect it from leaves, cats, and rain.

❖ Let your child help you with garden chores, or give him or her a small plot to care for alone. Choose quick-growing plants such as lettuce, beans, radishes, marigolds, or bachelor buttons.

❖ Go miniature golfing with your child early in the morning, when it's cool. It's a child-size play world.

Water Play

❖ Make a water pistol out of an empty plastic dish detergent bottle or a kitchen baster.

❖ Put a plastic swimming pool at the bottom of the slide on a hot day and let the kids slide down into the water. (Don't buy a pool bigger than one adult can empty alone!) Stick bathtub appliqués to the bottom to make it less slippery and to repair any obvious holes.

❖ Fill balloons three-fourths full of water, close them with twist ties so they can be used again, and toss them around the yard.

❖ Give a child a dishpan of water, add detergent, and let him or her whip up suds with an eggbeater. Or let your child dip a plastic six-pack holder into the solution and wave it in the air for lots of bubbles.

❖ Let your child paint the outside of the house with water and a big paint brush, or add food coloring to the water, and let him or her paint the sidewalk.

❖ Make a very small hole in the bottom of a can, attach it to your child's tricycle, and fill it with colored water. The child rides until the "gas" is gone.

❖ Fill a coaster wagon with water, then add funnels, a kitchen baster, and an eggbeater for water fun without dirt. If you can stand the mess, a mud hole in the corner of your yard will delight children even more than a sandbox.

❖ Let the kids wash the car. It may not be uniformly clean, but they'll have fun. Or let them wash trikes, bikes, or toys.

❖ Use a kitchen strainer to clean the water in a kiddy pool and get rid of grass, bugs, and dirt that have collected. To keep a blow-up pool from popping, place it on an inexpensive shower curtain on the ground.

Snowy Day Specials

❖ Use an old plastic baby bath-tub for a sled. (Punch a hole in the rim and attach a rope.) It won't go too fast, and the sides will keep a small child from falling out.

❖ Let a toddler use a whisk broom dustpan for a snow shovel. It's the right size and height.

❖ Teach the kids to play a

game of chase in the snow. Draw a big circle by shuffling through the snow, and bisect it two ways, at right angles. The players can run only on the lines.

❖ Or show them how to make angels in the snow by lying down spread-eagled and moving their arms up and down and their legs together and apart.

❖ Fill a plastic squeeze or spray bottle with water to which you have added food coloring, so kids can "draw" on the snow or paint a snowman.

❖ Put special marks on a large outdoor thermometer to let children know when they must wear jackets, boots, and other heavy clothing. (And also mark summer temperatures that are warm enough for picnics and water play.)

❖ Put a coating of petroleum jelly on kids' cheeks to protect them in cold or windy weather from frostbite.

❖ Put inexpensive rubber gloves on over children's knit gloves to keep hands dry when playing in the snow.

❖ Or spray fabric protector on mittens to help mittens stay dry and keep hands warmer.

❖ For the young ice skater, keep feet warm longer by cutting a slit along the bottom of a pair of large heavy socks and slipping the sock *over* the ice skates with the blade going through the bottom slit.

Too Cold, Hot, or Wet to Go Out

Many parents depend on the malls, local pet stores, and the like, when the weather is lousy. Here are some other options:

❖ Let the kids play with snow in the kitchen sink, or with *lots* of snow in the bathtub. Cover them up with raincoats worn backward or outdoor play clothes. (This activity is best at floor-washing time—things might get messy.)

❖ Help kids with a little experiment: bring a bowl of snow inside and show them how little water it makes when it melts.

❖ Make an indoor sandbox out of any sturdy box or dishpan and fill it with rice or used coffee grounds (hasten the drying process in the oven)—ideal for roads for little cars.

❖ Let the kids "skinny-dip" in the bathtub for a while before naptime or bedtime to get warm and sleepy.

❖ Give kids a chemistry lesson and a rainy day project. Dig out some dirty old pennies. Mix vinegar and salt together, and let the children use it on an old cloth to polish the pennies.

❖ Make edible play dough: ¼ cup smooth peanut butter, 2 Tbsp. honey, 2 Tbsp. powdered milk, and enough powdered chocolate drink mix so it's not sticky. Mix until it has a good dough consistency. Mold it into shapes, or roll it out and cut it with cookie cutters.

❖ Make edible finger paint: one small package instant vanilla pudding mix and ½ cup water. Mix well. Add food coloring to make different colors, or use chocolate pudding for brown.

❖ Accumulate small, inexpensive items in a "bored" bag of things to do on a rainy day, and keep the bag secret. Some things you might want to include are games, books, toys, and small snacks like little cans of fruit, pudding, or juice.

❖ Go to the public library and check out some activity or arts and crafts books.

INDOORS AND OUT

You can buy loads of expensive toys and equipment that are educational and fun for children to play with, and you can take your children places where they'll learn a lot and have a good time. But you can also supply inexpensive things for them to play with that will provide hours of fun.

Playhouses, Forts, and Such

❖ Drape a card table with an old sheet to make a playhouse that can be put up and taken down in minutes. Cut or draw windows and doors, and let the kids decorate the sheet by drawing flowers, shutters, and bricks with felt-tip pens.

❖ Use a large mover's carton or the big box from a household appliance for a playhouse. Cut doors and windows and let the children draw curtains, rugs, and pictures inside and shrubbery, shutters, and a doorbell outside. Remember that large cartons can also be forts, tunnels, trains, boats—imagination is the only limit.

❖ Make good forts out of couch cushions, if you're willing.

❖ Hang bedspreads, sheets, or blankets over chairs (hold them in place with spring clothespins) for a secret hideout.

❖ Make train or airplane seats for several children with chairs and stools from all over the house.

❖ Spread magazines or furniture cushions around the floor to make "rooms" and to use as stepping stones. Or use carpet squares for "magic carpets."

❖ Put an old mattress on the floor for tumbling and jumping to save wear and tear on chairs, couches, and beds.

❖ Make a dollhouse by attaching together four boxes of the same size, two up and two down. Cut windows and doors. Give your child scraps of cloth, wallpaper, or carpeting, and let him or her decorate.

❖ The puppet theater you buy or make for indoor activities can be used as a lemonade stand in the summer.

Games

❖ Make a "busy box" for a toddler or infant with things to spin, a bell to ring, a lock and key, a chain to rattle, knobs, and balls—all attached to a heavy cardboard box.

❖ Give an old shower curtain new life and map out on it, with a heavy felt-tip pen, a village full of roads and railroad tracks. A child can spread it out and play with cars, trucks, and trains on it.

❖ Give a toddler an empty paper towel tube and a round balloon for a safe, easy-to-use baseball game. Tubes also make good tunnels for little cars.

❖ Make a ball stand for plastic-bat-and-ball play by stacking two tennis ball cans. Kids have as much fun knocking over the cans as they do hitting the ball.

❖ Paint small, empty juice cans or eight-ounce plastic bottles, and let your child use them for bowling pins, with a small rubber ball.

- Get out a box of old clothes and let your child play dress-up. Use old receiving blankets for capes, skirts, and veils.

- Give your child scraps of wrapping paper, tape, and pieces of ribbon to play birthday party, wrapping and tying his or her own toys for presents.

- Play dice games with a little child who finds dice easier to handle than cards. You can make dice from gum erasers cut in half and decorated with the usual dots or your own symbols.

- Let children who can't manage cards hold them with spring clothespins. Or slip them in the flap slot of a box of aluminum foil or waxed paper.

- Tape strips of masking tape over the corners of boxes of games and puzzles *before* they break. And preserve board games, puzzles, and even book covers with generous coats of spar varnish, clear polyethylene paint, or clear contact paper. All will make the items easy to clean.

Playing Games with Children: Win or Lose?

Lose without cheating by using a handicap system that you devise. In checkers, for example, change sides every three moves. Or make a rule that no player can be more than one captured piece ahead.

Puzzles

- Glue small unpainted furniture knobs from the hardware store on puzzle pieces to make them easier for little children to handle. You can paint the knobs to match the pieces.

- Make puzzles by pasting large, clear pictures on heavy cardboard and covering them with clear contact paper. Cut with a matte knife or small saw into as many as 25 pieces, even for a preschooler, in distinctly different shapes, such as stars, triangles, arrows, circles, and squares.

❖ Keep puzzles from getting hopelessly jumbled by marking the backs of all the pieces of one puzzle with one color, another puzzle with a different color, and so on. They are easier to sort by the color on the back than by the design on the front if inadvertantly mixed up.

❖ Store puzzles separately in self-closing plastic bags.

Things to Unmake and Undo

❖ Remember that any appliance or gadget on its way to the trash pile offers fascinating possibilities for unscrewing, opening, taking apart, and even smashing.

❖ Check out garage sales for broken clocks, record players, or cameras to take apart.

❖ Let the kids participate in any dismantling project in the house or yard—taking down a wall, digging a garden, breaking up a sidewalk.

Cleaning and Repairing Toys

❖ Save yourself work by buying machine-washable stuffed toys and dishwasher-safe plastic toys.

❖ Clean and deodorize toys by wiping them off with a moist cloth dipped in baking soda.

❖ Shake unwashable stuffed toys in a bag with generous amounts of cornmeal. Brush out the cornmeal, and the dirt will come with it. Cornstarch or baking powder will work as well. Or use rug shampoo and a brush.

❖ Clean cloth dolls by making a paste of soap flakes and water, applying it with a toothbrush, and wiping it off with a damp cloth.

❖ Paint paper dolls with clear nail polish to keep them from tearing.

❖ Apply two or three coats of nail polish to pinholes in inflatable toys.

❖ Soak plastic toys that have gotten out of shape in hot water; then work them back into shape.

❖ Cut circles from a wooden broom handle; sand and paint them to replace lost checkers.

ARTS AND CRAFTS

Don't ask your beginning scribbler or sculptor, "What is it?" say those
who work with children in arts and crafts. Such a question puts a child
on the spot. Instead, talk about colors, thickness or thinness of paint,
interesting shapes. Save yourself trouble when messy work is to be done
by having your child wear an adult's old shirt with shortened sleeves.
You'll save yourself more trouble if you have a tiled floor or if you put
down a plastic rug runner or piece of linoleum in your child's "creative
corner." Vinyl tablecloths make excellent play cloths under children's art
projects. Covering the work table with an old sheet also makes cleanup
easy. And let your child use your old baby nail scissors for cutting. Their
blunt tips make them safe yet sharp.

Painting

Investigate free or inexpensive sources of paper: rolls of discontinued
black-and-white wallpaper for coloring; shelf paper; ends of rolls of
newsprint from your local newspaper; brown paper bags; even newspaper
want-ad pages, on which print is dense enough to paint over. Save diaper
and shirt boxes with white interiors and cut them up for painting on. Or
make a writing or coloring board by covering a piece of cardboard with
clear contact paper. "Erase" with a dampened tissue or paper towel. You
can remove an 8-by-11 photo-magnetic sheet from a photo album and
place it over activity book pages such as mazes. Your child can color
them in with dry erasable marker pens or grease pencils you find in office
supply shops. It makes activity sheets reuseable, because all you need is a
tissue to wipe away the colors on the clear plastic sheets.

❖ Make finger paint for kids with canned milk and food coloring.

❖ Or combine shaving cream, shortening, or even instant pud-
    ding with food coloring, and let your child paint on the shiny
    side of freezer paper or on a cookie sheet for gooey fun.

❖ Mix powdered paint with liquid starch instead of water to get a
    better consistency for beginning painters.

❖ Or make instant paint by adding a few drops of food coloring
    to a little liquid starch in a small container.

❖ Mix a little egg yolk, dry detergent, and food coloring to make a paint that will stick to a shiny surface such as glass, foil, or freezer paper.

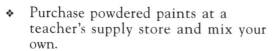

- Use food coloring and brushes to paint marshmallows!

❖ Avoid trips to the sink for hand cleanup by putting some paper towels and a spray bottle filled with water on the work table.

❖ Purchase powdered paints at a teacher's supply store and mix your own.

❖ When mixing paint with water, add a small amount of detergent. If the child gets paint on clothes, it will wash right out.

For Your Artistic Toddler

Let a toddler "color" right on the high chair tray with crayons. Later spray the tray with prewash and wash it in the sink.

Dishes for Paint and Water

❖ Use an ashtray with cigarette rests and double-suction disks underneath as a water dish—it provides a place to rest a brush and won't tip.

❖ Insert water or paint containers into holes you've cut in a big synthetic sponge to prevent tipovers and to soak up overflow.

❖ Use foam trays from supermarkets for artists' pallettes. (You can also use them to make airplanes that really fly!)

❖ Mix colors only in the amounts needed in small jars or foam plastic egg carton sections.

❖ A feeding dish with divided compartments makes a good artist's pallette for primary colors and water.

Personalized Hand Painting

❖ Make personalized "handprint" T-shirts as gifts or for kids to wear themselves. As a gift, have everyone in the family press their hand into fabric paint spread on a paper plate and then onto a white T-shirt. Write each family member's name next to the handprint. And use a different color for each hand. Or let children create a special T–shirt for themselves by having only their handprints in different colors on the front and back of the shirt.

❖ Make unique holiday cards by using finger-painted handprints on white paper. To make a flower, add a stem and leaves. For a turkey, add an eye and legs.

❖ Let the kids paint on the bathtub with water-based finger-paints. Afterward, just rinse the kids and the tub with water.

Brushes

❖ Let beginners paint with pastry brushes, which pick up a lot of paint. Or let them use cotton swabs or pipe cleaners with ends twisted into loops for painting that doesn't require fine line work. Even cut-up sponges can be used.

❖ Get brushes for toddlers at the hardware store. Brushes used for painting trim are wide enough and short-handled enough for them.

❖ Fill a cleaned-out roll-on deodorant bottle with paint and let the kids roll paint on.

Recycling Crayons

❖ Avoid arguments over using the basic crayon colors by buying a big box with lots of pretty shades and two extra boxes of the basic eight colors.

❖ Sharpen crayons by dipping them in hot water and rolling them to a point between your thumb and forefinger. Or use a vegetable peeler.

❖ Make "double color" crayons by removing the paper from two of the same length, melting one side of each over a candle flame, and letting them dry together.

Or bind three or four different color crayons together with a rubber band.

❖ Melt old crayon pieces (with paper removed) in empty juice cans set in hot water over medium heat on the stove or in baby food jars in an electric skillet filled with water. Pour the wax into the cups of an old muffin tin or into candy molds, cool, and unmold fun crayons for young children. Seasonal molds work great!

❖ Reinforce crayons or chalk by wrapping transparent tape around them.

Cleaning Up after Crayons

Remove crayon from a chalkboard using WD-40. On wallpaper use a piece of white bread to rub it off. On other places try to soften it first with a warm/hot hairdryer and then wipe off with a tissue. Or cover the area with brown paper and run a warm iron over it.

Glue

❖ Use liquid starch as glue for kids. It works well on tissue paper collages, cut-outs, overlays, or assembly work, and it dries overnight.

❖ Use up old clear nail polish as glue; the little brush is a good size for a child. Then refill the empty bottle with glue.

❖ Use an old plastic mustard container as a glue applicator.

❖ Put glue in one section of a foam plastic egg carton, and put small items to be glued—macaroni, beans, rice, or whatever—in other sections.

❖ Keep paste fresh and smooth by adding a few drops of water to it before closing the jar.

❖ Lubricate the cap grooves of glue and paste containers with petroleum jelly for easy opening and closing.

❖ Experiment with the colored glues available.

Storing Materials

❖ Convert an inexpensive cardboard shoe organizer into an art center for the floor or dresser top.

❖ Install a cafe curtain rod as a dispenser for a big roll of shelf paper for children's drawing and painting activities. Hang a pair of blunt-nosed scissors nearby so that children can help themselves.

❖ Use a kitchen cutlery tray to store art supplies and keep them separated.

❖ Poke holes in a block of styrofoam with one colored marker, and stand markers up in the block to keep them together and visible for color selection.

❖ Clean out an empty bleach bottle, cut away a section, leave the handle, and you have an excellent tote for materials.

Preserving Drawings

❖ Preserve a crayon drawing by putting it face-up on the ironing board (with newspapers underneath to protect the pad) and laying a piece of cotton sheeting over it. Iron the fabric firmly at a low to medium setting until the drawing has been transferred to the cloth, and let it cool before moving it.

❖ Spray drawings with hair spray to preserve the paper and keep the colors from rubbing off.

❖ Or soak special drawings in a solution which, it has been claimed, will give them "an estimated life of 200 years." Dissolve a milk-of-magnesia tablet in a quart of club soda and let it sit overnight. Soak the paper in the solution for an hour, drain, and pat paper dry. Weight corners down while drying. Move it carefully.

Your Artist on Display

Save artwork *you* like; let the kids keep the things *they* like; and encourage throwing away pieces no one especially likes. You'll cut down on the quantity of "keepers," and you'll be helping your children be more critical of their own work. Your praise will be believable, too.

❖ Reduce the clutter on the refrigerator by having each child choose his or her favorite picture to be framed in clear plastic. Date, sign, and display in the hallway.

❖ Let your child write notes to grandparents on the backs of drawings, saving paper as well as getting the artwork out into the world where it will be appreciated.

❖ Let your child make gift wrap by decorating white shelf paper with crayons or paints.

❖ Donate stacks of your children's artwork to a local nursing home. Let your toddler hand them out, and everyone will have a good time.

❖ Take pictures of your child standing by a display of his or her work posted on the refrigerator with magnets or displayed somewhere else. Later you can all look back and see the fine things created back then.

❖ Use a big piece of cardboard as a bulletin board to hang paintings on when the refrigerator door is full.

❖ Attach drawings to painted surfaces with a dab of toothpaste on each corner.

❖ Show your appreciation of a child's artwork by hanging a piece in the living room in a frame with an easily removable back. Change the artwork frequently.

❖ Save boxes that have a frame design, such as those from curtains, to hold and display children's art or keepsakes.

❖ Make placemats of drawings or paintings by sealing them between two layers of clear contact paper. Or insert them in plastic folders for changeable placemats.

❖ Use a clear plastic tablecloth and display drawings under it. Or, if you have a glass-covered table, slide artwork between the glass and the tabletop.

❖ Let kids paste drawings on formula cans, coffee cans, or other cans with plastic lids. They make great gift containers and are reusable as containers for art supplies and other small objects.

❖ Punch holes in drawings and save them in loose-leaf notebooks. Or let kids save the drawings they want by clipping them together with giant, colored plastic clips.

ENCOURAGING READING

❖ Attach some colored stickers to your child's different book/cassette tape sets so they can be matched correctly.

❖ Buy a special book for each child for each holiday occasion, as a family tradition.

❖ Keep your active child involved while you read aloud by letting him or her draw or paint. Or ask your child to bring a favorite toy animal along to "listen" to the story.

❖ Make audio recordings of your child's favorite stories to listen to when he or she is too tired to read. A tired child might like to listen to the tapes and just follow along in the book. Remember to say beep or ring a bell when you turn each page just as the commercial book-and-tapes do!

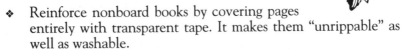

❖ Reinforce nonboard books by covering pages entirely with transparent tape. It makes them "unrippable" as well as washable.

❖ Schedule a daily reading time, whether it's during or after a meal, before a nap, or at bedtime. Make it a relaxed and fun time—not a chore.

❖ Reward older children with extra reading time alone in bed for a few minutes after the usual lights-out time.

PREPARING FOR SCHOOL

❖ Check out books from the library that tell stories about the first day of school.

❖ Visit the school, and let your child play on the playground equipment.

❖ Talk a lot about what school will be like, but be careful not to promise anything you're not sure will happen. Listen carefully to your child to discover fears and worries that may be lurking. Try to put yourself in the child's place. Some fears may seem silly to you, but they're very real to your child.

❖ Rehearse your child in reciting his or her full name, address, and phone number. Setting it to music can make it easier to remember.

❖ Try role-playing, and let the child play both pupil and teacher.

❖ During the week before school, see if you can take a walking tour of the school with your child. Ask to meet your child's teacher during the visit. You might even want to photograph the classroom, the cafeteria, and other important rooms in the school so your child will be familiar with the school on the first day of class. Go to an open house or "get acquainted day" if your school has one.

❖ Make sure your child has seen and used public restrooms so as not to be intimidated by the school bathrooms. Visit the ones at school. Make sure your child can clearly ask for bathroom privileges.

❖ Draw a big map including the home-to-school route, and put in major landmarks. Let your child play on it with small cars or dolls.

❖ Walk to the bus stop (or the school itself) with your child before school starts. Go over any special arrangements for returning home so your child truly understands the new routine. If your town has neighborhood safety programs, point out the "safe houses" to your child.

❖ New to the neighborhood? Is there a child in your neighborhood who will be walking the same route as your child? Introduce the children and allow them to get to know each other before the school year begins.

❖ Give your child two gifts to help with scheduling: an alarm clock or clock radio—and start setting it for bedtime and wake-up time—and a calendar on which to mark and cross off special days.

❖ Get school clothes together, and involve the child as much as possible in the selection of new ones.

Organizing for the Morning

❖ Set the school-night bedtime before school starts and stick to it. Get up early yourself, and get things going on the morning schedule you'll follow on school days.

❖ Start the routine of selecting and laying out the next day's clothes the night before, including shoes and socks. Have your child get used to dressing completely before breakfast.

❖ Set the breakfast table before going to bed.

❖ Periodically check that all clocks in the house show the same time.

Learning Left from Right

A child can form the letter L by holding up the left hand, fingers together, and thumb stuck out straight . . . and learn two things at once. Or, if the child is right-handed, he or she "writes with the right."

Off-to-School Routines

❖ Set a timer to help your child know when it's time to gather belongings and get ready to leave for school.

❖ Attach name tags to any clothes that will be removed at school—sweaters, jackets, and such.

❖ Tape milk money to the inside of your child's lunch bag or box so he or she can find it easily. Plastic sandwich bags work well to hold coins.

❖ Teach your child never to walk in front of the school bus unless and until he or she see the driver's eyes. That ensures that the driver will see your child, too!

❖ Supply your child with an empty paper towel tube for carrying important papers to and from school. In rainy weather, the tube can be slipped into a plastic bag for extra protection.

❖ Or get the child a regular school bag or small backpack—either is very grown-up. (And a backpack won't wear out from being dragged on the ground, as a bag will.)

❖ Keep old diaper pins handy to pin notes to the teacher on the child's clothing.

❖ Whichever parent usually goes off to work should drop the child at school the first few days. A child will be accustomed to saying good-bye to that parent, and it won't be so hard.

❖ Be sure your child understands that no one but a parent (or other designated person) can pick him or her up from school without written permission. Some families opt for a family password.

❖ Don't forget to inquire each day about school activities. Listen very carefully to the answers in order to head off any problems. (Some children will share more than others.) Don't give your child the "third degree"! You may find that the best time to ask about the day's events is at night, as you are tucking your child into bed.

Assuming you've now made it through (*and enjoyed*) your child's first five years, you now have the golden years, ages 6 to 12, to look forward to. These are the years when they are still young enough to adore us and old enough to release us from that tremendous job of physical caretaking that small children require. Enjoy these years, for beyond them is *adolescence!*

INDEX

Feed Me! I'm Yours

by Vicki Lansky

The best-selling guide to making fresh, pure baby
foods at home; over 200 recipes; lists of finger, fun
and birthday foods. Spiral-bound.

Order #1109

Free Catalog of Books by Vicki Lansky

For a free catalog of more than twenty books for parents
and children by Vicki Lansky,

call: 1-800-255-3379

or write: Practical Parenting
Dept. PPT
Deephaven, MN 55391

First-Year Baby Care
by Paula Kelly, M.D.

This handbook covers the first twelve months of life—when parents need help most! The step-by-step photos and illustrations make the up-to-date, authoritative information easy to use. This book covers bathing, diapering, feeding, first aid, child-proofing, and more.

Order #1159

Baby and Child Medical Care
edited by Terril H. Hart, M.D.

Step-by-step illustrated instructions for treating over 150 of the most common children's illnesses, injuries, and emergencies. Includes a symptoms index.

Order #1159

Discipline Without Shouting or Spanking
by Jerry Wyckoff, Ph.D., and Barbara C. Unell

Do you know all the theories about child rearing but still have trouble coping with some of your child's misbehavior? You'll love this book! It covers the thirty most common forms of misbehavior from whining, clinging, and talking back to refusing to eat, resisting bedtime, and throwing temper tantrums. You'll find clear, practical advice on what to do, what not to do, and how to prevent each problem from recurring.

Order #1079

The Baby Name Personality Survey

by Bruce Lansky and Barry Sinrod

This fascinating book is based on a national survey of 75,000 parents. It reveals the images and stereotypes associated with 1,400 popular and unusual names.

Order #1270

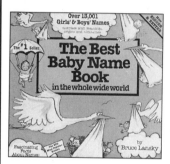

The Best Baby Name Book in the Whole Wide World

by Bruce Lansky

With over 13,000 names, complete with derivations and meanings, it has more contemporary names than any other book. No wonder it's the best-selling baby book in the U.S. and Canada with over 2.5 million copies in print.

Order #1029

Getting Organized For Your New Baby

by Maureen Bard

The fastest way to get organized for pregancy, childbirth, and new baby care. Busy expectant parents will love the checklists, forms, schedules, charts, and hints to make pregnancy less hectic. Maureen Bard, a university professor and mother of two, makes it easy for expectant mothers to get scheduled, budgeted, and prioritized.

Order #1229

Order Form

Qty	Title	Author	Order	Price	Total
	Baby & Child Emergency First Aid	Meadowbrook Creations	1380	$13.00	
	Baby & Child Medical Care	Hart, T.	1159	$8.00	
	Baby Name Personality Survey	Lansky, B.	1270	$7.00	
	Best Baby Name Book	Lansky, B.	1029	$5.00	
	Dads Say the Dumbest Things!	Lansky, B.	4220	$6.00	
	Do They Ever Grow Up?	Johnston, L.	1089	$6.00	
	Feed Me! I'm Yours	Lansky, V.	1109	$8.00	
	Getting Organ. for Your New Baby	Bard, M.	1229	$5.00	
	First-Year Baby Care	Kelly, P.	1119	$7.00	
	Hi, Mom! Hi, Dad!	Johnston, L.	1139	$6.00	
	How to Embarrass Your Kids	Holleman/Sherins	4005	$6.00	
	Moms Say the Funniest Things!	Lansky, B.	4280	$6.00	
	Mother Murphy's Law	Lansky, B.	1149	$4.50	
	My First Years Record Book	Meadowbrook Creations	3129	$15.00	
	Practical Parenting Tips	Lansky, V.	1179	$8.00	
	Pregnancy, Childbirth, Newborn	Simkin/Whalley/Keppler	1169	$12.00	
	Rub-a-Dub-Dub Science in the Tub	Lewis, J.	2270	$6.00	
	Working Woman's/Breastfeeding	Dana/Price	1259	$7.00	
				Subtotal	
				Shipping & Handling	
			MN residents add 6.5% sales tax		
				Total	

YES! Please send me the books indicated above. Add $1.50 shipping and handling for the first book and 50¢ for each additional book. Add $2.00 to total for books shipped to Canada. Overseas postage will be billed. Allow up to 4 weeks for delivery. Send check or money order payable to Meadowbrook Press. No cash or C.O.D's, please. Prices subject to change without notice. **Quantity discounts available upon request.**

Send book(s) to:

Name _____ Address _____

City _____ State _____ Zip _____

Telephone (_____)_____ P.O. number (if necessary) _____

Payment via: ☐ Check or money order payable to Meadowbrook Press (No cash or C.O.D.'s, please) Amount enclosed $ _____ ☐ Visa (for orders over $10.00 only.)

☐ MasterCard (for orders over $10.00 only.)

Account # _____ Signature _____ Exp. Date _____

A *FREE* Meadowbrook Press catalog is available upon request.
You can also phone us for orders of $10.00 or more at 1-800-338-2232.

Mail to: Meadowbrook, Inc.
18318 Minnetonka Boulevard, Deephaven, MN 55391
?) 473-5400   Toll -Free 1-800-338-2232   Fax (612) 475-0736